Miracles
From My Diary

Miracles
From My Diary

Pauline Harthern

First printing, 1984

cover design by Steve Wise

Library of Congress Catalog Card Number: 84-060307
ISBN 0-917045-00-9

Dedication

This book is dedicated to a truly remarkable man. Roy Harthern, my husband for 33 years, is my spiritual adviser and my very best friend.

Contents

Foreword ix

Introduction xi

1 A Father's Prayers Are Answered 15

2 Satan Flees the Household of Faith 19

3 God Turns Defeat into Victory 23

4 God Gave Me a Family 27

5 Gang Members Find a New Best Friend 31

6 My God Shall Supply All Your Needs 35

7 Meeting Jesus In the Wilderness 39

8 Prayer for an Underground Christian 43

9 Childlike Faith 47

10 A Marriage Made in Heaven 51

11 What Will You Do with Jesus? 55

12 Breaking Satan's Power over the Past 59

13 Baptized in the Holy Spirit 63

14 Overcoming Worldly Powers 67

15 Released from Schizophrenia 71

16 Ministering Angels 75

17 Changed by the Power of God 79

18 Freed from Fears 83

19 Hope for Homosexuals 87

20 Learning to Live in God's Abundance 91

21 The House Is No Longer Haunted 95

22 A Cure for Cancer 99

23 Speaking against Insecurity 103

24 Transformed by God's Power 107

25 The Christian Domino Effect 111

26 Conquering the Shadow of Death 115

27 A Baby Is Set Free 119

28 Great Miracles—Even in Little Things 123

29 What You Say Can Help or Hurt You 127

30 Raining on the Just 131

31 By Whose Stripes I Am Healed 135

32 Redeemed 139

Foreword

I find it very easy to recall the first time I met Pauline Harthern. I received an invitation to be a speaker at a women's retreat for her church in Orlando, Florida and readily accepted. When I walked in for the retreat, I was immediately greeted by an extremely pretty woman who had lovely warm blue eyes and a radiant smile—that was my first impression of Pauline.

Little did I realize that Pauline and I were to become such close friends!

Over a period of time, I began to notice that when we sat down and visited, she had a way of simply unlocking my heart. I found myself sharing so openly with her!

One time, I poured out my heart over a problem which I had experienced with my son, and I began to weep; I felt as though I could not stop crying. However, I was not crying from despair, but from what seemed to be a rejoicing in the Lord for His answer. I asked Pauline, "Why am I crying like this? I don't usually do this."

She had such a beautiful answer: "Well, the Lord just wants to do a warm and special work within you, Marilyn."

Pauline's answer is the key to her wonderful ministry. So many times when we have been together, the Lord wanted to do something warm, something special in my life.

That same beautiful ministry of seeming to unlock your heart and open up your spirit to the dealing of the Holy Spirit is one which flows easily into Pauline's writing. I've felt that same warmth touching my heart when I've read her articles in *Charisma* magazine—it jumps out of her writing. I'm sure *Miracles from My Diary* will be very special to you.

I've watched Pauline's life unfold before the Lord throughout these years; I've had the privilege of praying for her and being her friend. I've seen her face heartbreaking situations, and I've seen her overcome trials. But whatever is happening in her life, I know that she is a very precious member in the body of Christ.

We need members of the Body who are placed there for the purpose of warming our hearts. We need members in the Body who will open our hearts so that we can receive the warmth of God's love and His Word, and I believe that Pauline possesses that very wonderful God-given gift.

Pauline, thank you for being my friend, and for the many times and days without end when you have poured out prayers for me. Thank you for sharing your life so very openly with others, simply to encourage them in the Lord. God richly bless you in every step which you take to further the work of His Kingdom.

Marilyn Hickey

MARILYN HICKEY

Introduction

This is a book about ordinary people, everyday occasions, and real happenings. It shows God's great love for all of us and His miraculous solutions to our seemingly unsolvable problems.

In a few instances I've changed people's names to protect their privacy. But the facts are unaltered.

Who knows? One day you may meet Larry, the rice farmer from Beaumont, Texas, and learn more about how God protected him from financial disaster. Or Big Jim and his wife Linda, presently doing missionary work in Africa, may speak at your church and tell how God healed their broken lives. Perhaps you'll get to know Dorothy who was delivered from schizophrenia, and she can recount in even more detail how she discovered the power of the name of Jesus.

These people and others are in this book. And I'm in it too, telling how God has met and helped me have victory over many deep needs, the same as He will do for you.

Life isn't only laughter and singing. I am the daughter of an Assemblies of God minister in London, England, and I married Roy, the son of an Assemblies of God preacher from Stoke-on-Trent, England. In our early years of ministry we declared we believed in healing and deliverance and every blessing. Somehow, though, we did not know how to appropriate the miraculous into our everyday living. Certainly we did not comprehend spiritual warfare.

When something of a supernatural nature happened occasionally, we rejoiced — but pondered the unspoken question, "What about the many who still await their miracles?" Much of our interceding was a "begging" of a God who seemed unwilling to want to help us.

Hosea 4:6 states, "My people are destroyed for lack of knowledge." It never occurred to us to pull down Satan's strongholds.

Then one night in 1970 a dramatic change began in all our lives. I had been deeply distressed by the fact that many people had problems which prayer alone did not solve. I began arising each morning at 2 a.m., seeking God for answers in the only available place in our small parsonage, the bathroom.

One such time I found myself earnestly whispering to the Lord, *"Why are You so silent?* Something is terribly wrong. Either it is You or it is I — and I know it is not You. So what is wrong with me?"

In the silence and stillness of the early morning, God spoke, "I am going to lead you into a ministry that is entirely new to you but is certainly not new to Me." God then birthed a deliverance ministry in our lives.

Roy and I stood in awe and wonder as we immediately saw dramatic changes in the lives of individuals around us while we ministered God's deliverance. This set off a chain reaction of liberty throughout our congregation.

I began writing down these dramatic happenings in 1975 when Stephen Strang, editor of the increasingly popular *Charisma* magazine, asked me to write for the second issue of *Charisma*. He saw potential and encouraged me to write a regular monthly column which I did for eight years. I will always be grateful for his faith in me. He sensed the readership would identify with the everyday, complex problems of people who come to ministers or their wives in dire need.

As I wrote of God's miracles in my column each month, I received many letters asking me to "write a book." I consider myself to be first a wife, then a mother, then a minister's wife available to people, but certainly not an author. Those who know me would agree that I am an ordinary, everyday person seen at the Laundromat, the grocery store, and the beauty shop.

If you are anything like me, perhaps together we can see answers to life's problems in our glorious, supernatural, magnificent Savior who came to minister to ordinary, everyday people just like you and me.

I write this book with you in mind.

PAULINE HARTHERN

1

A Father's Prayers Are Answered

Three-year-old Bertie cuddled next to his father in the big feather bed. He slept there often now that his mother had passed away.

Some nights he stirred in his sleep as his father placed his hands gently on his head. "Lord, place my son into full-time ministry. Let him be a preacher of the gospel," he prayed.

Bertie's father, John, knew how to pray. He and his wife, Mary Ann, had attended the Wesleyan chapel on Sundays with their six children, Bertie being the youngest. During the week there were cottage prayer meetings and Bible studies.

The family lived above the fish-and-chip shop that John owned and ran in Lincolnshire, England. Mary Ann took care of the family.

However, the winter of 1893 was severe, and an influenza epidemic swept England. Mary Ann cooked enormous amounts of soup and carried huge bowls of it to her ailing neighbors. A frail, delicate little lady in her mid-thirties, she set out one blustery evening to deliver another meal to a sick family despite her own high fever. It was her last mission of mercy. Mary Ann died a few days later, leaving a motherless brood behind. Alice, the oldest daughter, became the "mother."

Bertie's father continued to trust the Lord. He walked five miles across fields, summer or winter, to attend prayer meetings. Sometimes Bertie was awake when his dad came to bed. "Son, we had a wonderful time tonight. We spoke in angels' tongues," he would say.

He daily went before God as prophet and priest of his family, praying specifically for each child. His heart's desire was that his children serve the Lord, marry believers, and rear God-fearing families.

Meanwhile, in the city of London, Lily, the youngest of five, was born in the family quarters above the large family-owned English pub. A nursemaid and servants cared for their needs.

Every day her father scrutinized the children's appearance before they left for school. "Heels," he'd bark, and five children would "about face" for him to inspect the backs of their shoes.

Lily loved music. Sometimes she heard the Salvation Army band playing during street meetings, and for some reason she would cry.

At other times her mother sang snatches of hymns made popular by the Moody-Sankey and Torrey-Alexander revivals. Again, a strange emotion would well up in Lily's breast.

By the time World War I came, Lily was a grown woman with a voice and beauty that were the envy of England. She was billed as "the most promising young singer in the British Isles."

She was worldly-wise but compassionate and often

went to hospitals, entertaining wounded soldiers with her marvelous voice.

There she met Bert. He had been wounded while fighting in France.

He was no longer an innocent boy under his protective father's care. Nevertheless, Bert's father's prayers continued for his son.

Bert's godly upbringing seemed so old-fashioned now. Yet he could not bring himself to go to a nightclub. He was uncomfortable at a dance, and drinking repulsed him.

But something about Bert's gentle, reserved nature attracted Lily to him. They began dating. Bert called Lily his "nightingale." She was soon taking lead parts in Gilbert and Sullivan operas.

When Bert married Lily, her father-in-law's prayers for his son seemed wasted. Lily loved Bert's father, yet a perverse streak made her pile on more makeup and act more worldly around him. John grieved over his daughter-in-law's actions but said nothing, preferring to take the matter to God in prayer.

Several years later Lily was at a dress rehearsal while Bert stayed home, looking after their baby, Barbara. Rehearsal finished early that night, and Lily decided to go home instead of attending the party given by the opera company.

Crossing the street to get a bus, she was arrested by singing. Pushing open the door to the Empire Theatre, she was shocked to find herself in a revival campaign. People were clapping their hands, smiling, and singing about Jesus.

"How utterly irreverent," she thought.

George and Stephen Jeffries conducted the revival. They were mightily used of God in healing the sick. People formed lines up to two miles long to get into their meetings. Lily saw men and women fall to the floor under the power of God. She thought they were fainting because of the large crowd and was disgusted by everyone's seeming lack of concern.

As she gathered her belongings and prepared to walk out, a man with a booming voice stopped her and asked, "Are you saved?"

"No, I'm not," she glowered back and swept out.

However, for several weeks "Are you saved?" kept flooding her memory. She wished it did not annoy her so. And then one night in another part of London she saw advertising concerning a revival campaign.

"I wonder if it is that same crazy lot," she thought, with a mixture of curiosity, disgust, and apprehension. "Maybe I'll just look in the door."

It was the same revival party. After entering, Lily heard a glorious tenor soloist. "I should get him for the opera," she thought. "Such wasted talent."

She sat down to hear more. As the service continued, Lily began to want what these people had. At the end of the meeting she stood with others to accept Jesus into her life.

Immediately, a great transformation happened within her. She didn't go to the prayer room for counseling. Instead, she ran home to tell Bert. She was afraid of losing Jesus.

"Bert, Bert," she said, shaking him awake, "I'm saved. I'm saved. You must go and get saved tomorrow, Bert."

His eyes grew misty as he thought, "To think she is telling me. Why did I never tell her?"

He did go. He did become a Christian. I was born to them two years later, and by the time I was four, my father was pastoring a church.

Grandpa John died before Bert and Lily were saved. But grandpa's prayers were answered.

2

Satan Flees
the Household of Faith

Something was wrong, drastically wrong. But what was it? Roy and I knew we had to discover the answer quickly if our church was to survive.

We agreed there was no finer congregation anywhere. Loving and generous, they gave us a new set of tires for the car and a new mattress and box springs for our bed. One Sunday morning as we mounted the back stairs to our apartment, we heard a clatter, the bang of the front door, and footsteps racing down the front steps. We entered our house and discovered a beautifully set table with all our favorite foods, steaming and ready to eat. We merely had to sit down and enjoy it.

Their lovingkindness often moved us to tears. It was a small church, and everybody seemed to accept everyone else, smiling with understanding at each other's idiosyncrasies. They loved the Lord, too, and many were old-time pentecostals.

Yet something was not right.

The church was unable to keep a pastor. My husband was the seventh pastor in nine years. Roy was only 25, and I was 22. It was our first church, and we were quite inexperienced, but the congregation constantly pleaded with us never to leave, adding that they were going to treat us so well we would never go anywhere else.

Sunday services were a problem. While everyone chatted before and after services, during the services a great depression settled on us all, and no one seemed able to say anything. We wanted to testify, but it was virtually impossible. In addition, no one had received the baptism in the Holy Spirit in seven years. Roy confided to me that when he preached, he had the feeling a metal band was being tightened progressively around his head.

One night I was alone in the church, putting out the weekly newsletter. Most of the people were out visiting new converts, the sick and elderly, or new visitors. I heard the front door of the church open and close. Footsteps approached the office. But no one was there. "It must be a ghost," I told myself, although I didn't believe in ghosts.

Several days later Roy had a similar experience. In fact, it happened so frequently when either of us was there alone that we accepted it as an unexplained phenomenon.

I went to the church to pray quite often. Sometimes as I was there alone, I became aware of footsteps— and then the feeling of a man in black standing behind me observing me. I would slowly turn and look, but there would be nothing there.

Roy and I wondered if it could be evil spirits. But we were scared of demons, and we thought they were only in places such as Africa or Asia.

Roy called the church to fasting and prayer for two weeks. Every morning and evening a prayer meeting was held at the church. We tried hard to battle through in prayer, but it was almost hopeless. Conversation flowed easily before and after each service, but it was as if a spirit of dumbness bound us at prayer time.

During my fast, in the early hours of the fifth morning, I awoke and heard myself speaking in tongues. A tremendous sense of the presence of the Lord filled the room, and standing by Roy was a brightness in the shape of a man. I was sure it must be Jesus. I shut my eyes — too awed to look into His face — and worshiped Him.

As I praised the Lord, I suddenly had a vision. I was walking into the church and thinking how nice the new drapes and the tiles looked. Next I was behind the communion table, feeling absolutely marvelous. The door behind the pews burst open, and a flock of vulture-like birds flew toward me.

"Don't be afraid, people," I shouted to the congregation. "These are demon spirits, and they are afraid of us."

With a power and vocabulary more like the apostle Paul's than mine, I hit my left hand with my right fist and commanded, "I adjure you in Christ's name, leave!" They turned and fled. Then another flock came in. My boldness and sense of well-being increased as I commanded them to leave. They did, but another invasion entered. After repeating this experience several times, I said, "People, rejoice, rejoice. They have all gone."

Then I was back in bed, praising God. I waited for Roy to wake up so I could ask him what he thought about my vision.

He took it very seriously; in fact, he told it to the prayer meeting later that morning. The congregation took it to heart. We joined hands and together took authority over every satanic force in Jesus' name. During that time I received the identical vision of vultures flying in to attack us and fleeing in defeat.

What a prayer meeting we had. And that night the church treasurer's wife received the baptism in the Holy Spirit. That was only the beginning of a move of God as people were saved, filled with the Spirit, and healed. Roy preached with great liberty, and people were gloriously free in the services.

Satan had been cast out of the household of faith.

3

God Turns Defeat into Victory

We had never before experienced a move of God like this. A real spiritual excitement pervaded the opening meeting. People were healed and saved.

What else would happen, we wondered as we left the service. We didn't know we were about to encounter a satanic attack to stop God's work.

Roy and I had traveled to Costa Rica in the spring of 1977, joining Elmer and Lee Bueno for a revival campaign in San Jose. The Buenos had been telecasting in Latin America for the PTL Television Network. They felt a campaign was needed and invited us to participate.

At first the only meeting place Elmer could obtain was a hotel convention room seating 300. However, after he prayed for a larger facility, a hotel suddenly became available which would accommodate 1,000.

The first meeting was a success. The following

morning Roy conducted a special service for ministers. Diana, a popular television personality who had recently committed her life to the Lord, gave the rest of us a special treat. She took us in her Volkswagen bus to the top of Irazu — a spectacular volcano.

While descending along steep, narrow mountain roads, we passed a community of little houses clinging to the sides of the road.

Suddenly, the brakes failed.

Diana pumped them furiously, but to no avail. She swerved into the right lane to avoid another vehicle and crashed head-on into a big milk truck that was coming up the hill.

I pitched forward against the steel frame of the seat ahead; a searing pain flashed across my chest. My left wrist "cracked," and it hurt to try to move my fingers. Pain flooded my hips and legs. Yet, to my own amazement, I felt full of joy. "Gloria Dios," I shouted over and over. Some people were weeping, but I was shouting "Glory to God" in Spanish even though I didn't speak Spanish.

Unable to account for my hilarity and praise welling up from within, I decided I was either dreaming or in shock. I came to the conclusion that if I were not dreaming, I was being rather obnoxious. People might be seriously hurt.

Three different people called Lee Bueno at the hotel, reporting our accident. Trying to piece the details together from their reports, she thought some people might actually be dead or dying. In truth, the injuries were minor.

I remained inexplicably excited. I refused to go to the hospital, although I was in pain and bruises nine inches long had started to appear on my legs.

Back at the hotel, Roy had been speaking about faith. At the precise moment of our accident, he opened the door to our hotel room, and God said, "Your faith will be tested right now." Then Lee brought the news of the accident, and it was an hour and a half before he heard anything more.

We finally returned to the hotel. Just as we arrived, a man drove up with a woman who was dying of cancer. Roy and another minister stopped and prayed for her right then.

Several hours later, in our hotel room, Roy discovered that one of my legs was shorter than the other. He prayed. The right leg lengthened. I felt better all over. At that moment the phone rang. The woman with cancer called and reported she was completely well and was preparing a meal for her family. We were amazed and excited and praised God together.

That night people packed the conference room, spilling out onto the stairs and into the hallways. At the end of the service Roy called Diana on stage. She sat in a straightbacked chair, and when he held her heels in his hands, he discovered that she too had one short leg, possibly resulting from the accident. While the people watched, God lengthened her leg.

Suddenly there was a stir. A former glider pilot, paralyzed from a plane crash several years before, and strapped into a wheelchair, made his way up the stairs to the platform. "When I saw God grow a leg, I knew He could heal me," he said.

He was completely healed.

The people surged forward to the ministers and wives on the platform for prayer.

Goiters disappeared, growths vanished, deaf ears opened. I stopped praying to watch one of the visiting ministers pray for a woman who had one brown eye and one white eye — with no iris or pupil. As I watched, a circle appeared, first pale blue then deepening until it was dark brown matching the other eye. "Thank you, thank you, I can see," she said.

These people had not learned to doubt and did not

know that we also were overwhelmed by what God was doing.

Finally, the crowd dispersed. Roy went to the room to change his shirt.

A mother brought her little boy about 9 or 10 years of age to me. "Leg short," she said in broken English. I prayed and almost panicked because it took several minutes for the leg to lengthen.

"Praise God. There you are," I said to his mother.

She shook her head, "Leg short, arm short." Eventually I got an interpreter who told me the boy had had polio and had one very thin leg and one very thin arm. He was wearing a long-sleeved shirt and long pants. I was going to pray again, but when I rolled up the sleeve and the pants leg, I discovered the arm and leg were normal! God had really been working during those few minutes.

Later, a report came concerning the accident. It was a freak thing. The brakes worked perfectly before and after the crash.

With 20-20 hindsight we realized Satan had tried to hamper God's work. God was revealing His glory in the meetings. Satan didn't like it. He planned to kill and to injure us in the wreck, thereby destroying the meetings.

Instead, God was victorious, and we grew in faith.

4

God Gave
Me a Family

It was Thanksgiving morning, but I didn't
have much to be thankful for. Roy was bringing me
home from the hospital after my fourth miscarriage.

The gynecologist said, "Pauline, I'm afraid you will
never be able to have children. You can't carry them."

"It's not fair, Lord," I thought to myself as I rode
home in the car. "I want children more than anything
in life."

The week I was in the hospital, I really believed God
would help me have this child despite the problems.
One of my favorite verses of Scripture had always been
Psalm 37:4, "Delight thyself also in the Lord, and He
shall give thee the desires of thine heart."

After all, I was the one who had created a doll family
when I was a child. I pretended I had four children
— a boy, twin girls, and a baby girl.

When I was a little older, I volunteered for babysitting jobs just to be with children. Later I became a first-grade teacher. Many Saturdays I donated my time to day schools and orphanages because I loved children so much.

Yet, the words spoken by the Hebrew children about to be thrown into the fiery furnace also challenged me, "If it be so, our God whom we serve is able to deliver us from the burning fiery furnace, and he will deliver us out of thine hand, O king. But if not, be it known unto thee, O king, that we will not serve thy gods" (Dan. 3:17-18).

"If not, Lord, I promise to be at peace," I prayed.

But I was battling a feeling of being neglected by the Lord. As I lay in bed at home recuperating, I flipped through the Bible, saying, "What shall I read?"

"Oh, Lord," I prayed, "I don't want to read about the children of Israel going around the walls of Jericho. I don't want to read about David and Bathsheba, nor Paul on the road to Damascus. Oh, heavenly Father, all this week I have talked to You, yet You have been so silent. I *know* You haven't forgotten me, but please somehow let me know You haven't forgotten me."

I picked up my closed Bible and casually opened it. I stared at Isaiah 49:15, a verse with which I was totally unfamiliar. The words almost seemed to be speaking audibly to me. "Can a woman forget her sucking child, that she should not have compassion on the son of her womb? Yea, they may forget, yet will I not forget thee."

I shut my Bible. My heart beat faster. I had just asked God if He had forgotten me. The verse instantly answered my question.

I opened my Bible again. This time my eyes fell on Isaiah 49:20, "The children which thou shalt have, after thou hast lost the other." I had never seen that verse before either.

"God, are You speaking to me?" I asked out loud.

Again I opened my Bible. This time when I looked

down, I read Isaiah 48:19, "Thy seed also had been as the sand, and the offspring of thy bowels like the gravel thereof; his name should not have been cut off nor destroyed from before me."

"Oh, dear Lord, You are talking just to me. Is there anything else that You want to tell me?"

My eyes were attracted to Isaiah 49:17, "Thy children shall make haste. Thy destroyers and they that made thee waste are gone from thee."

I began comprehending what was happening. God was promising me children. With tears of joy and humility I asked, "Lord, is there more?"

I opened my Bible again. It seemed determined to open to Isaiah again. I was astonished as I read Isaiah 49:21, "Then shalt thou say in thine heart, Who hath begotten me these, seeing I have lost my children, and am desolate?"

I thanked the Lord some more and looked at my Bible again. My eyes focused on Isaiah 49:25, "But thus saith the Lord, Even the captives of the mighty shall be taken away, and the prey of the terrible shall be delivered: for I will contend with him that contendeth with thee, and I will save thy children."

I couldn't believe this was happening. God was showing me verses I had never noticed before. He was applying them directly to my circumstances.

God had not forgotten me. He was very acutely aware of my problem. He was promising to give me the desires of my heart.

I couldn't wait for Roy to come home. I had great news. When he finally arrived, I told him everything the Lord had shown me. He agreed that God, indeed, had spoken to me.

"I think we should stop praying for children," I said. "We should start thanking Him for them because He's given us His Word."

For the next two years I praised the Lord for what He had promised me. Then I had a baby boy. Two and a half years later I had twin girls. A year and a half after that I had another girl. God had kept His word.

Now I had real children instead of the doll family I pretended to have when I was only a child.

5

Gang Members
Find a New Best Friend

"Help!" I was between a rock and a hard place and felt it was my own fault. I had been too confident, too self-assured, too cocky. Now I realized this was not enough; in fact, it was about to be my undoing. I could hear the clicking of my chattering teeth and feel my knees vibrating. "Get me out of here," I thought. "I want to go back home to America."

My dad died, and I had flown to England to attend his funeral and to be with my mother. My father-in-law was pastoring two churches at that time. I was asked to testify at a large rally on Saturday night, and I thought I did quite well. Then on Sunday I spoke for Dad Harthern at one church while he spoke at the other. At the end of the evening service, I had a nice, satisfied feeling. The congregation said they enjoyed hearing me.

Now I was at the other church in another city. For

four weeks now the church people had put on an additional service. They had been burdened for the local youths who were in street gangs. It was the month of November, a gray, chill, bleak month in England. To entice the young people into the church, hot tea and cakes were provided after the one-half hour service.

But it was not working out. In spite of all the prayer and love and food, it just was not working out.

"Pastor," some of the deacons said, "let's discontinue these meetings. These hooligans are destroying some of the property as they come in and out. Some of them jump over the pews. They are carrying knives and switchblades. Some are on dope. They are dangerous."

And they were aggravating! They refused to respond to any of the church people. Not "hello," not even "thank you." Stony silence greeted any attempt at conversation.

They were noisy, rude, vulgar, and rebellious. They entered the church each week with war-whoops and shouting and kept up constant heckling throughout the service.

I had not been forewarned. I was only asked if I would speak to the street gangs. Naively, I said yes.

The meeting had already started when I arrived. The church was packed. As I entered a back door, gang members were blocking my way. There was hardly room to breathe. Not only was every seat taken, but people were standing with arms crushed against their sides. The aisles and doorways overflowed with people standing wall-to-wall.

My father-in-law announced that before I spoke, a teenage girl would testify. I stood on tip-toe and strained to see what was happening.

As the girl went forward, gang members wolf-whistled, stomped, and clapped. They shouted obscenities, tried to grab her, and tried to trip her.

She "lost her cool" and told them to be quiet. More noise, whistling, stamping, and laughter followed.

She tried to testify about her conversion. She said she had once gone to taverns. "Yeah! Bring on the beer," the youths shouted. She talked about dancing before her born-again experience, and they yelled that they wanted to dance. Thankfully, there was no room to dance. But the verbal abuse, foul language, stamping, and whistling finally drowned her out. She sat down and began crying.

While she had been testifying — or trying to — I was overwhelmed by my own inadequacy. I knew I was not spiritually prepared. Cowardice linked up with guilt from a lack of prayer. I felt ill and knew I could not do it. I had nothing to offer these young hooligans.

Dad Harthern finally called for me again. Not seeing me, he called on someone else to testify "until she comes."

It was a repeat performance of the other testimony. Bedlam.

I knew I could not run. How could I let my dear father-in-law down? "Oh, God, please, please forgive me, and help, help, help me," I cried silently.

A great calm began coming over me. And a sense of relief, a sense of God's presence and power and, yes, "God-confidence."

Dad Harthern called for me again. I waved a hand frantically above the heads of the mob blocking the aisle.

I pushed forward to wolf-whistles, stamping, claps, and grabs while the workers tried to stop them. I did not know what would happen, but I knew it would be all right.

Then, to all of our amazement, especially mine, I started to laugh. I stood before them almost in convulsions though nothing was funny. When I finally stopped, the whole place was in shock and complete silence.

I hesitated momentarily, and a wolf-whistle pierced the air. I beamed at the boy who whistled and said, "Oh, thank you! I'm a 34-year-old mother of four children, and no one has wolf-whistled at me for years. Thank you. That will last me months."

This produced more whistles, but they were accompanied by smiles and applause.

"I'd like to take you home with me to America," I said. More applause. More smiles. (I hadn't planned to say any of those things, and it was quite out of character for me. It was as if a tape recorder were playing inside me and bypassing my mind.) I complimented those young toughs. Then, I told them about my best friend, Jesus.

We thought we would never get home that night. The ice had been broken, and those fellows wanted to talk.

Four weeks later, after I had returned to the United States, my father-in-law sent me the front page of the local paper. It was a report and pictures of these gang members exchanging their knives and drugs for Bibles.

Jesus had become their best friend, too.

6

My God Shall Supply All Your Needs

I fluffed and straightened my dress and glanced up at the road. We still had many hours of driving ahead before we would get to the ministers' convention. I hoped my dress would make it without too many wrinkles. Although it was four years old, it was the only really nice dress I owned.

I looked over at Roy, inspecting his attire. He knew how to dress. His shoes were nicely shined. No one would ever guess he had cardboard in them to disguise the holes in the soles. No one would know that his socks were darned either. And, unless they looked closely, people wouldn't see how frayed his shirtsleeves were. He kept his coat on most of the time anyway.

Roy's hair was combed neatly — just the way I liked it. His hands were handsome; his fingernails, just the right length.

"You look nice, honey," I said, smiling at him appreciatively.

"You do too," he replied and squeezed my hand. "Poor darling," he added. "Do you get tired of wearing that one dress? We need to get another as soon as we can. I don't know, with the four little ones growing out of everything so fast, there is never any money left for you and me."

"I honestly don't mind," I said. "Lots of people in the world have only the clothes on their backs. Nothing more. At least I have a couple of house dresses and a nice winter suit."

I tried to sound convincing in my answer. I thought again of 1 Timothy 6:6, "Godliness with contentment is great gain." But I had the nagging feeling there was more to God's will for us than that one oft used verse.

"Sometimes I wonder," Roy mused. "We tithe and are generous in offerings and to the needy. Does God want us to look like this? Look at us — we're a couple of ragbags! Maybe we should pray about it. Maybe some members of our congregation are embarrassed by us. I wish I had the money to dress you up like a doll."

I knew it troubled him at times that he couldn't provide more for us. I kissed him on the cheek. "Don't be worried," I said. "Our God will supply all our needs. If He thinks I need a new dress, I don't even have to pray. He'll supply. But maybe He thinks I don't need one. It's up to Him. I'm His responsibility because He bought me."

Roy laughed. "Well, we always ought to pray that we don't get in a wreck. I wouldn't want the hospital to see the state of our underclothes."

"My God shall supply all your needs according to his riches in glory by Christ Jesus" (Phil. 4:19). The verse stayed with me long after our conversation ended. Was it possible to walk in abundance after all?

During my personal prayer times in the days that

followed, I quoted the verse back to the heavenly Father. "Dear Father, I am so relaxed knowing that You supply all my needs according to Your riches in glory by Jesus. Therefore I will not worry ever again about needs," I prayed. "Concerning my one dress, if You think that I need another, I rest in the assurance that it will be supplied as well as all the needs of the children."

I continued to pray and thank God for supplying all of our needs. I reminded Him of how tired Roy and I had been and how much we would like a vacation. We had no money. If we were to have a vacation, God would have to supply it. I felt confident that if He thought we needed one, He would provide; if not, we would not have one. Either way, I would be content.

Finally, I mentioned a bill for $70 that was due the next Thursday. It was a need. Therefore, according to the Word, it would be supplied. "Father," I concluded, "it is so refreshing to talk over secrets with You and know that You'll decide what it is we need."

After we got back from the convention, an enormous box arrived via Greyhound. It was filled with exquisite, expensive clothes, just my size. A pastor's wife who was known for her beautiful clothes had gained weight. An explanatory note enclosed began, "Would you be offended if I offer you these clothes?"

Offended? I was overjoyed.

A lady, new to the church, approached me. "I am now working at a children's clothing store, and the Lord has laid it on my heart to clothe your four children totally," she said. "Is that all right with you?"

Thursday came, and we still owed the $70. I giggled to myself and waited for the mail. I had decided that that was how the money would be supplied. I was puzzled when no check was forthcoming and went back to God. "It's the deadline today, God. I know this is a need, and I thank You for supplying it. Isn't this exciting, Father? I know it will be supplied."

A little later the phone rang. It was from a bank in New Orleans, informing me that money had been deposited in my name. "Oh, no," I said, "I have never been there. There is some mistake."

Then they told me where the money came from. My father had died the year before. A small insurance policy had been processed through the New Orleans bank in my name. It was for $72.

On Saturday a letter came from England. Roy's father owned a tiny cottage on the Gulf of Mexico. He had rented it for the summer to some shrimp fishermen, but they had left without paying him the rent. "Do go to the cottage. It will be empty for five weeks," he wrote.

Our heavenly Father wants us to trust Him to meet our needs. At that period in my life I discovered just how faithful and gracious He is.

7

Meeting Jesus in the Wilderness

Roy and I had walked through wilderness experiences in the past. We knew the wilderness was not pleasant, but, like the children of Israel, we had to go through the desert to reach the land of milk and honey.

It seemed that whenever we accepted the pastorate of a church, we would have a wilderness experience for awhile. Each one of the churches was severely divided before we came; it took love, plus faith, plus fasting, plus prayer — but especially love — to get the church from the wilderness to "the Promised Land."

When we accepted the pastorate of our fourth church, the problems were more severe than usual, however.

Although there were many fine people in the congregation, there was also a faction of about a dozen families who were a continual source of discord. They

39

boasted that they had run off the last minister in less than a year. Some bragged they would run us off, too.

Even though we had been voted in by an overwhelming majority, this faction had already decided who they wanted as the next pastor. Of course, we didn't know this at the time.

Their plan was to freeze us out. They held weddings and funerals without inviting us and invited other ministers to conduct them. They met for private dinners and breakfasts and discussed strategy to remove us. At the end of the Sunday morning services, they left church immediately rather than shake hands with us or allow me to give them a hug at the door.

Throughout our first year at the church Roy and I pondered what to do. Several of those who were opposed to us came under conviction for their attitudes. They came to us and, with many tears, begged our forgiveness.

Not only did they confess their involvement, but they told us the leader of the opposition was conducting a smear campaign by spreading lies. Apparently we were weathering the storm so well that the leader had decided to step up the attack.

We confronted the leader, and he denied everything, reaffirming his loyalty. We confronted the other five couples still involved, and they denied it too.

Should we bring the matter before the entire church, we asked ourselves? This might reveal the truth, but we were concerned about the number of young converts who might be disillusioned.

As the pressure continued, I began feeling that everyone was against me. I felt bruised, battered, crushed, trampled upon. I became drained spiritually, emotionally, and physically.

I cried out to the Lord for His comfort and strength. I prayed that He would help me put things into the right perspective.

But nothing happened.

The days dragged into weeks; weeks became months, but the pressure didn't let up. Finally I could neither sleep nor eat.

Even my speech became confused — some words came out backwards. Roy was so concerned about me that he even considered leaving the ministry.

At that time Roy received two lucrative job offers. Both were Christian-oriented, and both were very tempting. Accepting either position would have gotten us out of our present dilemma.

But as we prayed about it, we knew we couldn't run from the ministry just because the situation was tough. Each of us had the call of God on our lives.

One Saturday morning I happened to be alone and went to the bedroom for my usual prayer time. I shut the door behind me and fell to my knees. I had prayed many hours in the past about the situation, receiving no answer. "Oh, Lord," I cried, "I really need You now as never before." I was desperate.

Just then the door opened, and an overwhelming sense of the presence of the Lord came over me. I knew Jesus had entered the room!

I had needed Him so long, and He had seemed so remote. There had been only temporary comfort in prayer or Bible reading — nothing personal, nothing permanent. Now He had come to pay me a personal visit.

"I trusted you in this place," He said to me. "I thought you could take it, that you wouldn't get discouraged nor give up. These problems aren't against you; they have been here for years. This is a stiffnecked, rebellious people. I shall not always strive with them."

("This sounds like something out of Exodus," I thought to myself.)

Then Jesus flooded me with love and compassion for His wayward children. And, He showed me what would happen to them if He lifted His hand of mercy.

I interceded with tears on their behalf.

I also felt grief for myself because He said over and over, "But I trusted you here."

Then the door opened and closed, and He was gone. I had been in His presence about half an hour.

He hadn't offered sympathy. Yet, I felt strangely comforted.

After that experience, Roy and I were able to cope beautifully. Later, when we left the church to take another pastorate, we did so because it was God's will for us to move, not because we were frustrated. And while we stayed at the church, God united many hearts in His love.

But for a small band of discontents, the outcome was different. God's hand was removed from them. They experienced divorces, business failures, and terminal illnesses. They had removed themselves from God's protection by willful sin and disobedience. They stayed in the wilderness.

8

Prayer for an Underground Christian

Heart attack! I sat bolt upright and gazed as the man across the aisle of the plane flailed around, fighting for his breath, wracked with intense pain.

Two stewards deftly removed his tie, his jacket, his vest, and his shirt and snapped the small oxygen mask over his nose and mouth.

Roy and I were flying home from Sweden where he had been speaking to pastors at the Church Growth International Conference.

Pastors from behind the Iron Curtain attended the conference. For a number of years I have prayed for every country behind the Iron and Bamboo curtains. I was thrilled to see the faces of these people for whom I'd been praying.

Approximately 100 pastors from four pentecostal denominations from Yugoslavia were there. Under Tito,

43

they were allowed a certain amount of religious freedom.

And now we were winging our way homeward. Roy and I were very tired, and the stewardess suggested we go upstairs and stretch out.

I was lying there with pillows and blankets, trying to sleep, when the man had a heart attack.

It was awful to watch. A few passengers including an American doctor gathered around and tried to help him.

Suddenly the man placed his hands together, pointed his fingers up, looked toward the ceiling, and yelled a few words in a foreign language. Was he calling on God for help?

I couldn't see him as people tried to help him. Then for a brief moment our eyes met. I put my hands together, pointed to myself, and then pointed upwards and mouthed, "I will pray for you."

Everything became chaotic. The airplane's captain had left the cockpit to confer with the doctor. The doctor said, "He has had a massive heart attack and needs to be hospitalized at once."

The pilot told him we were in the middle of the Atlantic Ocean. They discussed the alternatives.

The Lord said to me, "I want you to lay hands on that man in the name of Jesus." I pondered this, then got up and shut myself in the little restroom so I could be alone.

I said out loud, "Father, I will be happy to obey You and lay hands on this man and pray. Only I can't push my way in front of the doctor and those other people. Please let everyone leave so I can pray for him."

I opened the door.

Everyone was gone. The man lay perfectly still, eyes closed, breathing via the oxygen mask. I knelt beside him and gently tapped him. He opened his eyes, and I indicated non-verbally that I'd like to pray for him. He gave a weak smile, and I quietly placed my hands on his chest and softly began to rebuke the pain and the cause of the attack.

Suddenly he began to shake violently, and, a little afraid, I opened my eyes and looked at him. He was very vigorously nodding his head. He had a very big smile on his face.

I had noticed that I had used "in Jesus' name" repeatedly. In most languages it is rather similar. He must have understood that phrase.

I patted his cheek and smiled. He suddenly removed his mask and beckoned me lower. He began to sing in a whisper an old English hymn which I knew as a child, "Cleansing for Me." I joined in, although our languages were different. Tears filled my eyes. He was a believer.

"You go to sleep now," I said. I went back to my seat.

There was a noise from across the aisle once more. I watched in amazement as the man carefully put on his shirt, his tie, his vest, and then his jacket. Then he began combing his hair.

The doctor and the pilot bounced up the stairs. They had it all worked out. They stopped in amazement when they saw him.

As they tried to communicate, they discovered he spoke and understood French. They explained they were going to get medical help for him.

"Non," said the man.

"L'hospital, le docteur, l'ambulance," they insisted.

"Non, non, non," he replied. "Merci, mais non."

Finally, the pilot shrugged. "We might as well go on to New York then."

When they left, he came and sat beside me. We smiled and nodded. I wished we could communicate. I opened my purse and began to pull my New Testament out of it. He frantically waved his hands not to do it. "Non," he whispered. I looked up, and his traveling companion was coming up the stairs. They chatted briefly, and the friend went back downstairs.

"Parlex-vouz Francais," said the man.

"Un peu (a little)," I replied.

"Mon ami n'est pa (My friend is not a Christian)," he said and folded his hands as if in prayer. "Je suis," he said and again folded his hands. (I am a Christian.)

"Where are you from?" I asked in my dreadful French. "Hungary?"

"La Bulgarie," he said. We got the map from the pocket of the seat in front of us, and he pointed to Bulgaria.

His traveling companion was coming up the stairs again, and my new friend went back to his own seat. They were both looking at the map, and I heard, "New York, Miami," and then missed the final destination.

Who was that man, and where was he going? Did he have a wife and family? Can he only look at the Bible in secret and praise the Lord silently? He was so full of fear. Nevertheless, his heavenly Father was thoroughly aware of him. I'm sure he knows that. But just to confirm it, over the mid-Atlantic God healed him because he was special to Him.

I also remember my friend in my prayers although I can only say, "God, be with that man today."

9

Childlike Faith

He was such a dear little boy, about seven years old, with curly brown hair and blue eyes. He, his mother, his little sister, and I chatted together in the church prayer room for about 25 minutes.

They were a delightful threesome, and I enjoyed getting to know them. But as the mother explained why they were there, my pleasure dissolved. As she talked on, I inwardly panicked, although I tried to keep smiling and nodding.

"My reason for being here," she said, "is that I want you to pray for my son's eyes. You can see they are not straight, and it is affecting his vision tremendously. Glasses can't remedy this, and so we would like to have prayer that they will straighten." The trio was all smiles.

I smiled and nodded some more.

"Oh, dear God," I thought, "I don't have much faith. Why did I come in today anyway? Why did she come to me? This dear little fellow will be crushed if nothing happens. He thinks his eyes will be normal after we've prayed."

There were times in the past when I was shocked at my faith. I often looked back on situations and wondered at my own spiritual audacity and daring. I believed in miracles. I witnessed some staggering ones. But I somehow didn't feel a miracle would happen today.

The mother continued talking. "Eighteen months ago your husband prayed for our little daughter. Her eyes were very badly crossed. She did not receive an instant healing, but every time the doctor examined her eyes, they were a little straighter, until today they are almost normal. Although she still has to wear glasses, we are believing that they won't be needed for too much longer."

I was so glad she told me that. It took some of the pressure off me. If the little lad did not receive an immediate miracle, perhaps he would not be too crushed after all. He would keep believing for a more gradual but nevertheless definite healing.

An instant healing could happen, but if not, no one was going to be angry at God — or me. And I didn't suppose I would ever see them again (to have to check up on what did or did not happen in 18 months!).

I finally relaxed and stopped guessing what God would do. The child was God's responsibility. Only He could heal him.

The little boy was all smiles. His faith was strong. The little sister's eyes had been crossed inward. His eyes looked out to each side. We all closed our eyes. I prayed, rebuking blindness, weak muscles of the eyes, too strong muscles of the eyes, double vision, amblyopia, glaucoma, squinting — and anything else I could think of to do with eyesight! Then we asked our heavenly Father to straighten those eyes and to give perfect eyesight in Jesus' name.

We all opened our eyes and looked at the little fellow. The mother gasped. The sister gasped. The boy gasped. And I gasped. His eyes were perfectly straight. All of us started praising the Lord and thanking Him for a mighty miracle.

The little girl asked for prayer that her eyes would be totally normal. We prayed, and she took off her glasses. She said she could see.

The thought crossed my mind that perhaps she was only trying to make us all happy as her brother's healing had done. I kept watching both children's eyes to see if they would slip sideways again. But God's healing was bigger than my doubts.

Standing before me was a sweet Christian mother who had taught her children to believe and two little people who believed mama and therefore believed God.

I was so deeply moved by the entire experience that I was virtually speechless the rest of the day. Simple childlike faith. A childlike trust. The beautiful way that little children accept God's promises without worrying about what other people think. All that was needed was obedience to His Word in claiming a miracle.

My eyes had been opened too. I remembered the gentle admonition, "Come to God as little children."

10

A Marriage Made in Heaven

Although I had shed a few tears in secret, I took a deep breath and gave a large smile to our daughter Suzanne as she came down the aisle on the arm of her father, kissed me, and presented me with a rose. She was a beautiful bride about to marry evangelist Benny Hinn.

Memories flooded my mind. I remembered 16 years before when our four children were pre-schoolers. I told them the story of Samson and Delilah (although I left out some of the gory details). I emphasized that Samson's problems came because he loved a girl who did not love God.

Four solemn faces looked up into mine. It was a special moment. I finished the story and prayed for each child and his or her future partner. Roy and I began to make this a regular prayer request.

Benny Hinn was about ten years old then. He lived

in Tel Aviv. He was Greek Orthodox and attended a Catholic school. Later, in 1967, he immigrated to Canada, was converted, and began to be mightily used of God. We had no idea that he was the one for whom we were praying — for Suzanne.

As the children grew older, instead of preaching to them, we tried to convey messages in subtle ways. I placed a five-by-seven picture frame by the telephone. Every few days I would place a different saying in it: "It is never right to do wrong and never wrong to do right," or "A sweater buttoned wrongly in the beginning will also finish wrong."

One day, years later, when she was in college, Suzanne confided in me because she was confused about what to do with her life. She did not want to be a secretary, a nurse, or a teacher. She didn't even know what she should major in at college.

Jokingly, I said to her, "Do you want to be like me — a nothing?"

"You're not a nothing," she answered. "You love the Lord, dad, your children, and your home. And you are used of God, mom. You go around speaking, counseling, and praying for people. I think I'd like that."

So, during that summer as I traveled, Suzanne served as my chauffeur and prayer partner. One day I reminded her that if she were looking for a handsome prince to come into her life, he would also be looking for a princess.

Suzanne had always fasted and prayed and read her Bible. But now this intensified. I also noticed that her messy room and untidy car were now clean and neat. The blue jeans and T-shirts she had worn were replaced by feminine dresses. Hair care, skin care, diet, and vitamins became important to her. And even though the dentist said it was a borderline case, she decided to wear braces.

She was becoming a princess for her prince.

I knew each of my three girls had very high ideals.

Each wanted a husband with the same high standards. They wanted a husband who had not gone from girl to girl, who did not tolerate rock music, and who put pleasing God first in his life.

One day my godly mother confided in me, "I was praying for Suzanne today, and I felt the Lord say she will marry Benny Hinn."

As much confidence as I have in my mother's spiritual insight, I could barely believe that. "Oh, mom," I said, brushing aside the comment, "you don't even know Benny Hinn and neither does Suzanne."

Shortly after that a series of incredible incidents took place.

First, Benny came to our church to hold services and afterwards asked shyly if he could spend Christmas with us. We said of course he could.

I told my girls I was glad they weren't boy crazy so that Benny could relax while he was in our home.

"Please don't fall in love with him. A lot of girls do, and I don't want you to be hurt," I told them. So, they treated him courteously but casually.

We did not know then that Benny had prayed, "Lord, I need a wife," and had presented the Lord with 23 qualifications for the girl he wanted to marry.

While he was with us, Benny was mentally checking off the list. Suzanne met every criterion he set.

Later, Benny held a meeting in California. The pastor teased Benny by asking the congregation to pray for Benny to find a wife. After the service, in the pastor's study, Benny said, "I have found the girl I am going to marry."

"Who?" the pastor joked.

"Suzanne Harthern."

The minister was silent, then said, "Benny, I feel the witness of the Spirit to that. I think you're right."

That's not all.

Benny introduced Suzanne to some friends who took him aside and told him, "We think she will be your wife."

We met Benny's father soon after. "My wife has seen Suzanne in a vision," he said. "She knows her name, age, and coloring."

A few weeks later international Bible teacher Derek Prince and his wife Ruth came to minister at our church. Derek laid hands on Benny and Suzanne and prayed for them. Afterwards, he said, "I'm sure God is in this. Such an anointing came on me. It was more an utterance of prophecy than of prayer."

As I saw Suzanne walk down the aisle, my tears were tears of nostalgia and reminiscence, but they were also tears of joy and rejoicing for God's wonderful plan for my daughter.

As we pray for our children's future, marriages can be made in heaven.

11

What Will You Do with Jesus?

It was New Year's Eve. My mother and a friend braced themselves against the biting wind and carefully made their way along icy streets. They were going to the traditional watchnight service in a little pentecostal church in London, England.

Suddenly a lone woman appeared. "Lily, Lily. Where are you, Lily?" She weaved crazily across the snowy road. "Lily? I want Lily."

"She'll get herself killed," my mother said.

The woman continued, staggering and reeling and calling Lily.

"I'm Lily," said my mother, going to her and tucking the drunken woman's arm through hers. The woman lurched against her, trying to focus her eyes on my mother's face. "No you're not. You're not Lily."

"Oh, but I *am* Lily," mother assured her, "and I will take care of you."

The two godly women half carried her to the church.

Mostly she slept, but when the soloist began to sing, "What will you do with Jesus?" she suddenly became angry. "Haven't you got anything better to do?" she shouted.

At 3 a.m., the service over, mother brought her home. There was nothing unusual about that. We never knew whom mom would bring home with her.

Actually, we discovered Phoebe had a fine husband and daughter and son-in-law. She was very rebellious concerning spiritual things, yet at the same time she couldn't stay away from the church.

She showed up at street meetings, beer bottle in hand. My mother had a glorious voice. She had given up a very promising career in the operas when she became converted. Phoebe listened sullenly each time until mother stepped forward to sing.

"Come, sinner, come.

Salvation's free for all.

It may be the last time

You hear His call."

The singing always infuriated Phoebe. "Can't you shut up? Haven't you got anything better to do?" she'd shout.

Mother's speaking also angered her. Yet she would follow mom as she went from church to church, speaking at women's meetings.

One day a furious Phoebe came to our home.

"Who told you all about me?" she demanded. "Just how much *do* you know?"

Puzzled, my mother said she did not know what she was talking about.

"Yes you do," Phoebe said. "This afternoon at the Congregational church you spoke about Hannah and Samuel. You were telling the people all about me."

Mother reassured her that she knew nothing about her.

One day the women at our church had a special day.

There was an afternoon meeting followed by a tea. Phoebe baked a delicious cake. One minute she was loving, the next hostile; kind and then critical; reaching out a little and then withdrawing — and always watching mother and smirking, "Haven't you anything better to do?" Lizzie Hyde, a wonderful woman of God who was converted when she was a girl working in the Lancashlie cotton mills, was the speaker. The Spirit of God rested greatly upon the meeting, and the women decided to have another service after tea.

Very informally, before the service began, Lizzie suggested that before they sang the hymn, "He Rescued Me," each woman read one of the verses as her personal testimony.

Phoebe was in a dreadful state as her turn came. Her face contorted, she struggled to say, "Haven't you anything better to do?" But instead the tears came. It was as if the "fountains of the deep were being broken up."

"Once I was wayward,
Afar would stray.
His wondrous Grace
Has rescued me.
"Now I'm on
The King's Highway;
A brand from the burning,
He set me free."

Then Phoebe crumpled to her knees and sobbed, "Be merciful to me, O God. Forgive me. Forgive me."

"Lily," she later asked, "what shall I do? My life is such a mess. Years ago I was a very active Salvation Army lass. My husband went away to war, and I was unfaithful. I gave birth to a baby boy who died at birth. Every week I go to a certain hotel and pay blackmail so my husband will not find out. I've done this for 30 years."

"'Fear hath torment' but 'the truth will set you free,'

Phoebe. Don't pay another payment, and don't be afraid to tell your heavenly Father — or your husband. Humble yourself before them, and don't be afraid," my mother told her.

The truth did set Phoebe free. It destroyed walls of rebellion, fear, torment, tension, and so many other emotional harassments. Phoebe had sung "What Will You Do with Jesus?" many times in the Salvation Army. Now she knew the answer.

"What will you do with Jesus?
Neutral you cannot be.
Someday your heart will be asking,
'What will He do with me?'

"I'll take Him home with me.
I'll take Him home with me.
That's what I'll do with Jesus;
I'll take Him home with me!"

12

Breaking Satan's Power over the Past

"Satan, in the name of Jesus, you are commanded to let go. You cannot continue to harass this child of God with his past. You are trespassing, and we give you marching orders. Right now, loose your grip from his life. In Jesus' name your power is broken, your plans are smashed, you have no control whatsoever. We will accept nothing more from you."

A few minutes earlier I didn't know I would be commanding Satan to release his grip from Bill's life. But as Bill shared his problem with me, I knew strong action was needed.

Bill was one of my favorite young people; he had come to the Lord with a whole-hearted surrender and a genuine sorrow for his sins. He grasped spiritual truths quickly and put them to work in a practical everyday way.

This particular day we happened to meet in the

hallway of the church. I was on my way to do some volunteer counseling; he had stopped by to pick something up. We exchanged hellos and how-are-you's, and then he expressed his concern about one of the young people who had become deeply involved in drugs. I had been very disturbed about it too.

"Pauline, how I wish I could get through to these young people," he said. "If they get busted, their whole lives are ruined. I know from experience."

"What do you mean?" I asked. I did not know from experience and did not understand. "Why would their entire lives be ruined? I mean if they come to God in repentance and receive deliverance and trust in God's mercy, won't God release them as He does all backsliders who are truly sorry?"

"What these young people don't know," he replied, "is that once a person has been arrested for drugs, it is recorded on his permanent record. Wherever he goes, it follows him. Every time he applies for a job, his bad record will thwart his getting it, and he will never be able to establish credit."

"My goodness, I didn't know that."

"Oh, yes," he continued. "I'm speaking from experience. I came out of college and had a very fine job. I was earning up to $15,000 a year. But I was also heavily involved in drugs. I was busted and jailed. My record is with me everywhere I go. Every job I've applied for, I get turned down. I don't suppose I will ever be able to earn more than $100 a week. I'll always have to be content with menial jobs. This also means I can never buy a house, and, of course, I'll never marry because I couldn't support a wife and family. This is what young people don't realize. They just don't understand."

"That's terrible." I was a bit shocked, and I stood mulling over his conversation. I looked at him for a long moment and then said very deliberately, "Well, I don't believe it, and I won't accept it. Oh, forgive me.

I mean, I do believe all that you've told me regarding the facts. But I also believe that because you are a child of God, Satan has no power over your life. I don't think he can hold you guilty of your past any longer."

He laughed ruefully at my naiveté and shook his head. "Pauline, you have obviously not applied for one job after another and had your record nullify your every effort."

"What would you choose to do if you could select your own job?" I asked.

He laughed some more, but as I persisted, he became serious.

"Well, there are several jobs I'd like. I've applied for a personnel job, but the one I'd like most is a sales job. Oh, but I'd never have a chance."

"That's the one we'll claim." I was elated.

"I believe Satan has to let go when we command him to. And according to John 16:23 if we ask the Father anything in Jesus' name, He will do it. In Mark 11:23 we are told that we can have what we say. Let's do those things now."

We did. We cut him loose from his past record, we asked for the choicest of jobs in Jesus' name, and we praised God that we had the job we were claiming.

Several days later I was again at the church. A sudden urge to pray for my friend came to me. I prayed and claimed God's promise for quite some time.

Two days later he came back to the church. Before he could say anything to me, I asked him what he had been doing two days earlier at 10 a.m. when I was praying for him.

"I was having a job interview at that exact time, and I got the job," he said excitedly. "Praise the Lord."

Later, Bill married a lovely girl and bought a home. Bill's past could not deprive him of God's blessings for the present and future.

13

Baptized
in the Holy Spirit

"She's speaking in Polish," the lady missionary at the youth camp said.

She was referring to me. I was in my mid-teens.

It was August 1945. For a year I had delivered newspapers every day at 4 a.m. and had cleaned houses on Saturdays to save money to attend camp.

And now, after one of the evening sessions, in the bedroom of the farmhouse where I was staying, my friend and I had asked the Lord for the baptism in the Holy Spirit.

I sensed God's presence filling that little room in the Derbyshire Hills. Then each one of us was immersed in the Holy Spirit.

From midnight until after 2 a.m. I was lost in the Spirit. My hands were raised that whole time, yet I was not tired. All the while, I spoke in another language. And the missionary said it was Polish.

Finally, the farmer's wife tucked us into bed, but I could not sleep. I spent the night very quietly worshiping the Lord in another language. Oh, the feeling of cleansing. The nearness of the Lord. I had experienced intimate communion with the Lord of my life.

As I rejoiced in the Lord the next day, I discovered that if I did not really concentrate, I spoke in tongues to people instead of English.

After youth camp ended, life gradually returned to normal. Sadly, nobody explained to me that the Holy Spirit had given me a prayer language, a new dimension in worship, a new weapon in intercessory prayer, a way of daily personal edification.

Nor did anyone explain to me how subtle Satan is. He is a thief who comes to steal, kill, and destroy. And he does not try to steal from people who don't possess anything. But to the possessors of salvation he says, "Are you sure you're saved?" To the person healed, "You are not really healed; it will come back." And to the newly baptized in the Spirit, "That was only you. You made it all up."

So, in spite of the rapturous experience I had had, I believed Satan's lie that I had made it all up. I was further convinced that I had now committed the unpardonable sin and would never be forgiven.

Our congregation had many activities, and I participated in all of them—street witnessing, slum work, visiting orphanages, witnessing in taverns, and holding street meetings. We would pray and fast and work. We had great times of rejoicing, and then I would remember, "I have committed the unpardonable sin." I was tormented by the thought.

The Sunday morning services were strictly for believers and included a time of communion and worship. One by one we stood and worshiped the Lord. Often, when my turn came, I felt overwhelmed by His presence and love. A tremendous feeling of "fullness" possessed me. My neck and mouth felt somehow "blown up." I had great difficulty trying to get words to come out correctly in English. In the middle of a sentence, I'd abruptly say amen and sit down.

Fear would overtake me; I was not sure God had forgiven me for what happened that summer in youth camp. "Such blasphemy," Satan said, "making it up, and then saying you had the baptism in the Holy Ghost the same way it happened on the Day of Pentecost."

For two years Satan buffeted me. I constantly asked for God's forgiveness and promised that never again would I utter a word in anything other than English unless I could not help myself.

That was a pretty tall order.

On a bitterly cold winter's day the fire had gone out in the potbellied stove at the church. Nevertheless, a small crowd gathered for the weekly communion service, and as the stove was relit, we huddled together for warmth.

Various ones began to tell what God meant to them. They lifted their voices in praise and adoration to the Lord. When my turn came, I became more and more aware of His greatness and nearness. The feeling of fullness began. It was very hard to speak. I frowned as I concentrated on trying to finish a sentence. The words kept vanishing from my mind. With great difficulty I determined to complete a phrase, say amen, and sit down.

Suddenly I began stuttering. I struggled to talk. Then, immense release swept over me, wave upon wave—like the fountains of the deep were being opened up. Soon I realized that someone was very noisily gushing forth in another language. Those sounds came from me!

God had supernaturally given me an experience I could not doubt. How clean I felt. And how hot the building was, even far away from the stove. People were removing their topcoats, and even sweaters and jackets, and were all joining in the wave of blessing and rejoicing.

I no longer had to worry that I was making up the language. And the experience was not a figment of my imagination. I was with God's people in the same type of atmosphere the 120 must have encountered on the Day of Pentecost, described in Acts 2:1-4.

I did my part by opening up to God. And He was faithful to do His part, filling me with the precious Holy Spirit.

God always finds a way to meet those with seeking hearts.

14

Overcoming
Worldly Powers

Intercessory prayer is not popular
with many Christians. But those who are engaged in
spiritual warfare know it is one of their most powerful weapons.

Pastor and Mrs. Stanley Sjoberg of Stockholm,
Sweden, unleashed this weapon against the satanic
powers opposing them and their beloved country. The
results were miraculous.

Christians in Sweden are very aware of the condi-
tions in the various East European countries. They are
also conscious of the strategic position in which they
are placed between communism and the free world.
They spend much time in intercessory prayer on
behalf of their own country and also for their immediate neighbors.

"Intercessors for Sweden," an international prayer
organization which has similar branches in many

other countries, including America (Intercessors for America), meets the first Friday of each month for fasting and prayer for the entire nation.

Some time back, when it seemed that the communist party would become a majority in the Swedish parliament, the churches began fasting and praying. God gave Pastor Sjoberg, through a vision, insight as to what was happening in the country. He shared this with his congregation.

A government official heard of this and secretly visited Sjoberg. "Where did you get your information?" he inquired.

"From God," Stanley replied.

"Only five people know this information," the official told him. "It is top secret. What are you going to do about it?"

"We will pray for God's will," Pastor Sjoberg replied.

Almost immediately the Sjobergs became the target of harassment. They received constant threats on their lives. He was given bodyguards everywhere he went.

One night his wife and four daughters were alone in the house, unprotected. The phone rang, and a voice said, "We know that you and your children are alone in the house. Tonight we are coming to kill you."

"Really!" Mrs. Sjoberg replied. "I'm excited about it. I shall look forward to your coming."

"Madam, you must not have understood," the man said. "Tonight we are coming to kill you and your children."

"Praise God," the spunky minister's wife exclaimed. "You mean that tonight my girls and I are going to meet Jesus? I'm delighted. I'm thrilled. This is our whole reason for being and the joy of our lives. Oh, praise God. When will you be here? I can hardly wait."

"You are insane. Why are we wasting time on you?" sighed the exasperated voice at the other end of the phone. That was the last she heard from *them*.

The Sjobergs' church continued to grow and soon were in desperate need of a new building. However, the local government officials violently opposed it. The key official was a socialist and very opposed to the Church.

The congregation regularly prayed concerning this situation. One day the elders of the church were praying, and a spirit of intercession came upon all of them. One of them said, "As we pray, let us visualize ourselves in the power of the Holy Spirit going into the chief opponent's office, laying our hands on his head, and asking the Holy Spirit to cause him to cooperate."

They did this. In a relatively brief time the whole situation totally changed. The chief official cooperated fully, granting every permit they needed to build the new auditorium.

To minister to the various needs of the local people, the church developed what it called a "charismatic clinic." Christians who know how to intercede give their time voluntarily to help the needy, the sick, and the distressed.

A woman who had been blind for six years came for help. She had been suffering from severe depression and wanted to be set free. As the group began praying, she suddenly cried out, "I can see color! I can see the color of your tie." Rapidly, everything took clear shape, and her vision was perfectly restored.

In the midst of her rejoicing, sadness flickered across her face. "I have a son in America who has the same disease as I had. He too is totally blind. Could we please pray for him?"

The group immediately began to pray, breaking the bondage of this sickness.

On arriving home, she went to the phone to call her son and share the exciting news about the restoration of her sight. Before she could do so, however, the phone began ringing. It was her son.

Both began talking at once. She wanted to tell him the great news. But he had news to tell her. At almost precisely the same time, he had also received his sight. On both sides of the Atlantic they rejoiced.

The Sjobergs have taught their congregation the power of intercessory prayer—whether to change the course of a nation or to restore sight to the blind.

How God longs for us all to use this great weapon.

15

Released
from Schizophrenia

Driving home after ministering in a near-by city, Roy glanced over at me and said, "That woman is crazy."

I had to agree. Dorothy's wild antics had disturbed the entire meeting.

When Roy started giving a closing prayer to those gathered around the front of the auditorium, she cried out, "I'm dead. I died in 1967."

Quickly, the pastor of the church went over to calm her.

She would not be quieted. She grabbed him, ripping his shirt. Others tried to restrain her, but she wrenched out of their grasp. She looked frail but had uncommon strength.

After several minutes Dorothy settled down, and the pastor asked me to take her into another room, away from the people.

I did as the pastor requested and silently prayed for the Holy Spirit's protection, wisdom, and knowledge. Dorothy might be dangerous.

"Are you a Christian, Dorothy?" I asked, trying to establish some common ground. She didn't understand my question.

"Have you ever asked Jesus to come into your heart?" I asked her.

"How could I?" she responded. "I don't have a heart. Oh, yes," she continued in answer to my puzzled expression, "you see, my heart turned to stone in 1967."

"I am talking about giving your life over to Jesus," I explained, "letting Him be Lord of your life."

"You don't understand, honey," she patiently answered. "I died in 1967. I know I'm dead. I have seen myself in my casket in the grave many times."

I asked her to tell me all about herself.

She rambled on about police and fires and stone hearts and death in a family she couldn't remember clearly. Nothing made sense. Her eyes gleamed with delight as she told me how she had schemed her escape from the Central Florida mental asylum to which she had been committed for life. Her story was fascinating and very clever. She might be insane but she was cunning.

After considerable time, I convinced her in her more lucid moments that God had not brought us together to waste our time or His. In fact, I was able to lead her in the sinner's prayer and to assure her that now her life was committed to Him. He was responsible for her every need and would help her.

Several Sundays later as I stood greeting the people in the church vestibule, I saw her again. "What are you doing here in Orlando and how are you?" I asked and hugged her.

She needed help, she said. It was obvious that she did. She would "come and go" as she talked, slipping in and out of insanity. I felt I was conversing with more than one person.

"Come back on Tuesday at ten and we'll pray together," I suggested.

Tuesday we met in the prayer room, and almost immediately she began to berate me. "My left side is all bad. My right side is all good. Everyone always pulls on my bad side. No one ever helps the good side. Why did you never help me?"

"I want to help you now," I said gently and reached my hand toward her.

"Don't you touch me," she shouted. "You'll lock me up. I know you." And she disappeared around an alcove and hid among the choir robes hanging there.

I buzzed my husband on the intercom. "Could the ministers give us an hour? I need all the faith we can muster."

Within minutes, my husband, three associates (one of whom did not believe in deliverance), and two housewives joined me. We agreed in prayer, commanding insanity to leave, ordering manic-depression, madness, idiocy, vacancy, and other insane spirits to go also.

Dorothy suddenly shot out of the chair where she had been persuaded to sit and landed on the floor. We didn't touch her, but we praised God that in Jesus' name these spirits had to leave. She pounded the floor and screamed at the top of her lungs.

Then she stopped and in a surprised voice asked, "Whatever am I doing on the floor?"

We helped her back to her seat. I hugged her. "Jesus is setting you free, Dorothy."

"Shall we deal with the schizophrenia next?" I asked the ministers.

Don, the new associate who had not believed in deliverance, suddenly knelt at her chair. With tears streaming down his cheeks and a voice broken with emotion, he said, "Dorothy, Jesus is the answer. I had a brother who was schizophrenic. He went to a minister for help at three in the morning, and the minister told him he had no answer. 'Go to a psychiatrist,' he said. My brother was discovered dead the next day, having hanged himself."

We were all in tears as Don then proceeded to command the schizophrenic spirits to leave. Once again Dorothy landed on the floor. She started banging her head violently against the wall, but the spirits were commanded to be still in Jesus' name and not hurt her or us. The roots of schizophrenia—rejection and rebellion—were ordered to leave one at a time. The former left with great sobs; the latter, with screams. Loneliness, despair, suicide, hopelessness, violence, hatred, resentment—all were told to leave in Jesus' name.

Finally, all the ministers except Don left because of prior commitments. I also had other people coming in for counseling. At the end of the afternoon, I saw Don and Dorothy coming from the prayer room. She looked so transformed, so radiant, that I did not recognize her immediately.

"She has received the baptism in the Holy Spirit," he said. "And now she is going to be baptized in water."

I wanted to leap for joy. "Oh! The Lord has been busy today. Look what He has done for you," I said.

Satan had been defeated again in spiritual warfare. Dorothy was a "new creature in Christ."

16

Ministering Angels

"Hello, boys," I said when I came back from the store and opened my front door.

Two teenagers returned my greeting and quickly hurried outside.

Moments later I understood their rush. The house was a shambles. They were not friends of our children as I had assumed. They were thieves.

We never saw them again nor recovered the stolen goods.

But more importantly, how could I prevent others from robbing us in the future? "What about angels?" I thought. "They could protect us."

I remembered that Hebrews 1:14 talked about angels as "ministering spirits, sent forth to minister for them who shall be the heirs of salvation." And Psalm 34:7 states, "The angel of the Lord encampeth round about them that fear him, and delivereth them."

I decided to ask for an angel to protect our home. Months passed, and a rash of burglaries occurred in the neighborhood. Each time our house remained safe.

I also asked for angels to go with me on trips and to take care of my luggage. Prior to this it was not unusual for me to arrive at an airport to fulfill a speaking engagement, only to have my luggage delayed at my last transfer point. Now, however, even when I ran to make connections, my luggage made it too.

On a trip to Spartanburg, South Carolina, I sat by a very spry, alert, intelligent 73-year-old gentleman. A successful semi-retired businessman, he made frequent trips from Palm Beach, Florida, to Spartanburg. As we waited to take off, he told me many interesting things concerning textiles, dyes, and clothing. But as take-off time drew near, he became extremely jittery and ordered two stiff drinks.

"Honey," he said to me, "as much as I travel, I have to admit I'm really scared of flying. I'd never survive without a couple of drinks."

I reached over and held his hand. "You needn't be afraid today, Mr. Ferguson. Nothing will happen to this plane as long as I'm on it. I'm a child of God, and I always ask for His angels to travel with me."

We chatted some more, and he seemed to relax— whether from the drinks or the angels I didn't know.

"Honey," he said suddenly, "when are you returning home?"

"On Friday."

"Well, I sure hope I get on your plane," he said.

On Friday as I sat buckled up to fly into Atlanta, who should be beside me but my friend. "Mr. Ferguson, good morning," I smiled. "Remember the angels."

"Oh, honey, yes," he replied. "I won't be needing a drink today."

Divine protection is good for more than planes and

homes, I found out after I flew from Orlando, Florida, to Springfield, Missouri. I went there to bring back my daughters Suzanne and Leanne from college.

Springfield was in the middle of a blizzard. For three weeks it had snowed and iced over some more. The car we were to drive home was encased in ice and snow. It was difficult to recognize it among the others that had been left there over the holidays. Some of the ice on the car was five inches thick. After getting the door open, we prayed the car would start. After some coughs and sputters, it did.

Several college girls helped us load my daughters' belongings into the car. And we headed to a motel.

Six more inches of snow were predicted that night. At the motel we prayed that this would not be and on waking saw that a light, powdery snow had just begun.

We started the car. It made an embarrassingly loud squeal as long as the gas pedal was pressed. "Power steering? Fan belt?" We tried to guess what might be wrong. We pulled into several gas stations only to discover they were not open. Springfield was like a ghost town. We found one station open, but it was closing.

"But it's only 10 a.m.," we protested.

"I'm sorry, ma'am. We don't even have any gas," the operator replied.

A severe blizzard was now predicted for several days. We discussed the prospect of starting a 1300-mile drive with tires unchecked, less than one-half tank of gas, and something squealing.

I phoned Roy. "I don't think you should come," he said. "If the car breaks down, you could freeze to death and not be found for days. But, it is really up to you."

Shocked by his words, I phoned the highway patrol.

"Ma'am, we make no provisions for the roads," an officer told me. "They are treacherous. Arkansas is worse. It is going to worsen. Only a few trucks are braving it. I will not advise you, but your husband is right. You could be found dead in several days by the roadside."

The girls and I talked the situation over. For some reason we were not afraid.

"Let's spend several minutes and ask the Lord what to do," I suggested. In a little while we looked at each other and smiled. "Let's go."

We phoned Roy again. "Please pray and get others to pray. If we have your O.K., we are coming home."

We then asked for angels to clear the roads, guide the car, protect us from being in or causing a wreck. We prayed over fan belts, tires, steering wheel, and nuts and bolts.

We pulled onto the highway. Our route was clear of snow and ice. Yet, according to radio reports, other routes were not. Fifty miles out of town we were able to purchase gas. From Springfield to Memphis, Tennessee, we saw several trucks but only two other cars.

Three days later we arrived home. Leanne took the car to the local gas station to wash it and fill it. One tire disintegrated and another went flat! A report stated that 55 people died in the blizzard in the Midwest that weekend.

I am glad I know about ministering angels.

17

Changed
by the Power of God

There it was again—the eerie whistle of a speeding train. Only this time it was considerably closer.

Hiroshi readied himself. Deliberately he walked to the edge of the tracks. Distraught, depressed, diseased, and disillusioned, he simply wanted to end his life.

With a thunderous roar the train sped toward him. He closed his eyes and prepared to jump. How he welcomed death.

Buddha had never helped him in the past. Hiroshi didn't even believe in him anymore, or any other god for that matter. It would be easier to be dead.

But moments later Hiroshi opened his eyes and saw the now retreating train. It had not hit him. He was still alive. Some unknown power had held him back from jumping into the train's path.

He felt like a bigger failure than ever. "I'm unable

to live, and I'm unable to die," he thought.

Hiroshi Nishihara had not always been a failure. And there had been a time when Buddha worship was a very important part of his life.

He had been born into a poor family in Matsuyama City in Shikoku Island, Japan. His family had a little "Buddha box" to which they brought offerings and worshiped Buddha.

Intelligent and ambitious, Hiroshi studied hard and at 19 entered the Osaka university in the Foreign Languages department. His dream was to learn English with an American accent, immigrate to Los Angeles or San Francisco, marry a beautiful but tiny American girl, become very rich, and then bring his family to the States. This would be pure happiness, he thought.

When the "All Japan Intercollegiate English Oratorical Contest for the MacArthur Trophy" was announced, Hiroshi entered and came in second place. He was happy because his dreams were becoming reality. He was proud of his successes and was confident of becoming a prosperous businessman in a foreign trading company.

Hiroshi now began having breathing difficulties but thought the problem was due to too much studying and not enough rest. But it was soon diagnosed as tuberculosis of the left lung.

Hiroshi had no money and was therefore unable to go into a hospital. He tried to continue working to pay for his tuition. His condition worsened, and for four years he struggled to stay at the university. Finally he was forced to drop out.

Life became unbearable. He turned to alcohol, gambling, and street fighting. He became a hoodlum, completely bound by vice. His one compelling desire was to die.

He earned some money tutoring students in English. But what he earned, he squandered and still considered himself a failure. Now he attempted suicide and even failed at that.

As days passed, some pesky questions began intruding his thoughts—Is there life after death? If there is, then where would I go?

"These questions are ridiculous," he told himself. "I'm an atheist. There is no God. There is no life after death." But the questions continued to haunt him.

One day one of Hiroshi's students told him of a man who taught English for free. Hiroshi couldn't understand why anyone would offer such a valuable commodity at no cost and decided to investigate.

He sat in on the man's class. It was taught by a missionary from Texas. He was teaching the Bible in English. Hiroshi didn't want to stay but was too polite to leave.

As he listened, he became more curious. What was it that made Christians so different? They were kind and had joy in their lives.

Hiroshi wanted what they had. "Dear Jesus," he prayed, "come into my heart. Forgive me of my sins."

Immediately something changed. Not only did Hiroshi feel clean inside and out, he also discovered he could breathe normally. He was healed.

Hiroshi's life changed course. He now helped the missionaries and felt better about himself. And one day as he prayed, he received another language. He was baptized in the Holy Spirit. At that point he felt God calling him into the ministry.

He was elated, but when he told his wife Kimiko, she said she would leave him and take their son and daughter with her. She was not going to live a life of more poverty and sacrifice.

Shortly after that, Kimiko became violently ill. For three days she lay paralyzed and had a raging fever. It was apparent that she was dying. No doctor could help. In desperation Hiroshi hurried to a church where believers were gathered in prayer. They interceded on

Kimiko's behalf, and when Hiroshi arrived home, he found his wife completely healed and committed to the Lord, to him, and to the ministry.

Hiroshi and Kimiko surrendered their ways to the Lord and spent much time in prayer. Hiroshi had been changed from a failure to a man with a purpose in Christ.

Today he pastors the largest pentecostal church in Japan.

18

Freed from Fears

My heart hammered in my ears. Beads of perspiration formed on my brow. I felt I couldn't breathe.

Looking left and right in the dim light, I saw the glowing exit signs on each side of the auditorium. I mentally calculated the distance and route from my seat at the front of the church to the nearest door.

I felt panicked.

"Ridiculous," I chastised myself. "Forty-two years old and afraid of the dark. Nothing changes when the lights go out. It doesn't affect the air I'm breathing. The people in this church still breathe whether it's light or dark."

I didn't consider myself a fearful person normally. In fact, at times I was almost naively brave. I took the dogs for a walk at 2 a.m. some mornings. I enjoyed praying while strolling through the neighborhood.

At other times I simply forgot to lock the doors when Roy was out of town.

Once I stopped a huge man who was chasing his little wife around the house, trying to kill her with a knife. "You great big bully! Put that knife down at once," I said without a second thought.

But here I was now with a terrible fear both of the dark and of closed-in places. It was a fear of not being able to breathe.

My fear of the dark possibly began when I was about 11 years old and lived in London, England, during World War II.

During those days we knew what it was to suffer daily loss. Our church was razed during a bombing attack. Our school suffered a similar fate. Our home was constantly blitzed.

When I attended a new school, we met in underground shelters shaped like long tunnels. There we did our lessons and ate lunch. During one bombing run, a blockbuster dropped at the entrance of the shelter. It did not explode. All the lights went out. We sat in total blackness. Hours later the bomb was defused and the electricity came on. We finally got to go home.

After I was married, I began to feel the need for "just a chink of light" during the night. I said it was "in case anyone got up who was not quite awake."

My fear of closed-in areas first manifested itself when I was about 20 years old. I tried to take off my pencil-slim, long-sleeved black dress but forgot to unclasp the hook and eye at the neckline. I started to panic and felt trapped as I wrestled with the tight dress and tried to free my arms.

Years later when I needed surgery to remove a possibly cancerous growth from my throat, everything went well. I didn't fear the operation or the biopsy. And the growth turned out to be benign.

However, when I regained consciousness after the

operation, I discovered that both hands were band-aged to the side bed rails. And my throat was heavily packed and bandaged. Tears rolled down my cheeks as I pleaded for the nurses to set me free.

My fatherly and compassionate doctor was close by and, with an understanding which the nurses did not comprehend, loosed my hands and put just a light gauze over the incision on my throat.

As the years passed, my claustrophobic fears were terrifying. I wondered if I would become a maniac if I ever became trapped or tied up. I was thankful I had sympathetic doctors who insisted during the birth of our four children that I could be trusted and that my hands and feet were to be free in spite of the nurses' objections.

Roy and I taught our children not to fear people, thunderstorms, mice or bugs, or situations with the enemy. But eventually they became aware that I could not go through car washes and preferred to walk flights of stairs rather than to go via elevator.

I tried, I really did. I bought a number of small flashlights—one for each purse, reinforced by mat-ches should the batteries fail. I prayed and strengthened myself by repeating Psalm 34:4, "I sought the Lord, and he heard me, and delivered me from all my fears."

I quoted Psalm 56:3, "What time I am afraid, I will trust in thee."

"In fact I will trust and not be afraid," I said. But I was. "Just don't be like your silly mom," I told my children.

Now, years later, I was panicking as our associate pastor gave an illustrated sermon and dimmed the lights.

The church suddenly went darker. I started to scrab-ble around in my purse. The flashlight. Small as it was, if I could see its tiny glow, I could make it.

Then 2 Timothy 1:7 flashed through my mind. "God

hath not given us the spirit of fear; but of power, and of love, and of a sound mind."

"The spirit of fear. Is that what I'm battling?" I became very indignant. Why should I have to put up with any spirit from the devil?

"You spirit of fear of the darkness, fear of choking-claustrophobia, in the name of Jesus get out," I prayed silently yet angrily. Anger at the devil for fooling me into thinking it was a psychological hang-up all these years. Anger that he'd dare to invade the temple of the Holy Spirit. Anger that he'd take advantage of a child. But then, why should I ever expect him to be fair?

As my prayer ended, I became calm. My breath was no longer erratic. I made it through the rest of the service with no problems.

At a missionary rally the following evening, the film broke, and we sat in the dark for several moments. It didn't bother me. At our home, soon after that, Roy absentmindedly snapped off the bedroom light, stranding me in a dark closet. There was no panic. No problems with car washes and elevators either. The deliverance was a complete one.

Fear had to leave this believer.

19

Hope for Homosexuals

"I am a homosexual." He stood looking at me, his face contorting and his eyes downcast. His voice reflected a mixture of embarrassment and shame.

My heart went out to him. How I admired him for his honesty. "Joe, let's sit down and talk a bit," I said. "Pull up a chair."

It was at the close of a Sunday night service. Joe, in his early twenties, married and the father of two children, had asked to talk to me in private. He had been a member of my "Pairs and Spares" adult Sunday school class for the past two years, had given his life to Christ, and had been baptized in the Holy Spirit.

Since his early teens he had been very involved with his male cousin. Even after marriage his liaison had continued, camouflaged as hunting or fishing trips. But when he became a Christian, his conscience plagued him, and he knew the relationship must end.

The desire was still there, Joe said, but by praying, reading the Bible, and avoiding the cousin, he was almost making it.

"But every few months I slip up," he said as he wept. "Then I have such remorse, such hatred for myself; I'm terrified I'm going to hell, yet I can't help myself. This thing is too big for me to handle. I'm overpowered."

I had always dreaded the thought of a homosexual coming to me for help. I knew that Jesus was the answer, but I'd never seen one helped through prayer.

But now I called Roy in from his office so that he could help me.

Joe's problems were common to many homosexuals —an ineffective, henpecked father and a domineering mother who still controlled Joe and his father.

Roy discussed Joe's past and present problems with him and then commanded a warped, perverted spirit of homosexuality to come out of Joe in the name of Jesus.

In utter amazement we watched as Joe dropped to the ground on all fours and began barking like a dog, all the while expelling great streams of mucus. After 20 minutes he got up, drained, but happy. "I feel so clean," he repeated over and over.

About a month later Cindy, Joe's wife, came to see me. "Joe's and my relationship is not good," she said. "I take the blame. I think it is because when I was just a child my own mother led me into perversion."

I prayed deliverance for her. Her reactions were different from Joe's, but her feelings of release and cleanliness were the same.

"Will you tell Joe?" I asked.

"No, I won't," she said. "And, please, Pauline, keep my confidence."

"Of course," I agreed.

Every so often I checked with each one privately. "How's it going?" I asked.

"Just great," they assured me. I finally quit asking.

About 18 months later, Joe pulled me aside one day. He looked terrible.

"I slipped again," he said.

"Why?" I asked in disbelief.

"Well, since my deliverance all desire and compulsion left. Cindy and I were doing just great. But I went to a family reunion, and my cousin was there—and it just happened. Pray for me, Pauline, please pray for me again," he begged.

"Of course. Let's go back to the prayer room," I suggested.

I was perplexed. How had that thing dared to return? What right did it have?

"Joe," I said slowly, "does Cindy know anything at all about your problem?"

"No, Pauline. I don't want her to know either," he said.

"Joe, if this were not a spiritual battle, what I am going to say might not matter. But I wonder if you and your wife will ever be truly one or if you will ever have complete and permanent victory if we do not consider this," I said.

"Right now, Satan does have a foothold. You have been unfaithful to your wife, but she does not know. You and Satan have a secret. This gives him certain legal rights to harass you. I cannot take the responsibility for telling Cindy, but I think we should pray about it," I added.

Several weeks later I saw Cindy.

"Joe told me," she said. "At first I hated him. I even decided to divorce him, but then I suddenly realized that I wasn't much better. I went away for a few hours, calmed down, and sorted things out. Then I went home and told Joe about me. Then it was his turn. He despised me.

"Oh, Pauline, it was dreadful," she said. "But suddenly we found ourselves in each other's arms, crying and asking forgiveness. There is such a calm and peace in our hearts now. And such pure love for one another."

That was several years ago. Joe and Cindy moved to another city recently, but until the day they left, they both said that things between them were "just great."

20

Learning to Live in God's Abundance

When Roy and I were first married, we were advertized by churches as "honeymooning evangelists from England." For about three years we thoroughly enjoyed traveling from state to state and occasionally to another country. People were exceptionally kind and very generous to us.

Finally, we felt led to settle down in a pastorate. Again, we were surrounded by kind people, anxious to help.

We have now pastored five churches. We loved the congregations of each church, and they loved us. One underlying frustration was always with us, however. We were never able to get ahead financially. We were careful to tithe and were generous with our offerings. We did without rather than get into debt. Meals were carefully planned so as not to exceed the weekly $19 food budget. We deeply appreciated the fact that

91

people would give us furniture and clothing which were no longer of any use to them. In fact, we couldn't have survived had people not been so kind to us.

But our problem was uncanny. Although we had learned to be content living, at one time, in a two-bedroom cottage with no screens on the doors or windows, no heat, and certainly no air conditioning, earning $60 a week "if it came in," over the years it seemed that things were becoming progressively worse. Oh, we made more money, along with everybody else, but *our* baby would be allergic to milk and have to have expensive substitutes, *our* car would be a complete lemon. I remember a time when every appliance, big and small, from the iron to the refrigerator was not working. And as fast as we could get them repaired, another part would break down.

A church called us to pastor it. Having no parsonage, we borrowed a down payment and bought a home. We later discovered everyone around us had moved into their homes with no down payment. We smiled ruefully at each other and said "typical."

Struggling desperately, we added a playroom, a family room, a patio, drapes and rug, and a fence to augment our modest home to accommodate our family which grew from three to six people. Everyone who could helped with labor and said how the value of the home had increased.

Several years later when we were to pastor in another city, the economy was so bad that we could not sell, only rent at the price we were paying for the house payment.

Almost at once our payment increased. Now we were struggling to keep our heads above water. A small, inexpensive part went wrong with the oven, but a brand new oven had to be bought, for that particular model had been discontinued. The roof developed a leak. Then other holes were discovered. We were shattered to learn that it was not covered by insurance because it was hurricane damage which is "an act of God."

One day we just let the house go for the $11,000 still owing on it. A year later it was sold for $28,000.

Financial problems continued to plague us. One morning Roy and I discussed some verses of Scripture such as John 10:10 where Christ says, "The thief cometh not, but for to steal, and to kill, and to destroy: I am come that they might have life, and that they might have it more abundantly." We read 3 John 2, "Beloved, I wish above all things that thou mayest prosper and be in health, even as thy soul prospereth."

We wondered out loud whether the problem all these years was that Satan had robbed us. Right there we commanded Satan in the name of Jesus to give us back every penny he had stolen from us.

At once the miracles began. Purchasing living room lamps for the first time ever, the salesman suddenly said, "You can have them for 20 percent less."

The same thing happened when I purchased an item for the foyer. I stood open-mouthed while the store owner insisted on giving me a considerable discount.

I'm a pretty ordinary person, and having a mink stole never entered my head, but one evening after service a new convert draped one over my shoulders. "The Lord told me to do it," she said. I tearfully stammered thanks but protested that I thought she was acting out of impulse and that I couldn't possibly accept so generous a gift. "When I was earning $100,000 a year as a nightclub singer, I bought five stoles. God told me months ago one was for you," she said.

Living in God's abundance was an exciting adjustment. As the flow came in, we passed it on. As we passed it on, more came in. The years of faithfulness in finances to God and man did not go unnoticed.

You can live in God's abundance.

21

The House Is No Longer Haunted

"Family Flees Home in the Middle of Night," the Halloween eve front-page headline of our Orlando, Florida, newspaper read. A young couple with two preschoolers was experiencing strange phenomena, the article said. They believed their house was haunted.

One of the little girls woke up frequently during the night because a "voice" called to her. The father would sit in a chair, and it would be pulled away by an unseen being. Ashtrays floated away from him. The two dogs in the yard whimpered and howled piteously and trembled with fear. No amount of persuasion or bullying could induce them across the threshold of the house.

But the young woman was the most afraid. She believed, as they all did, in the supernatural. But she was extremely psychic, having amazed local authorities concerning unknown details in regard to a murder committed in a nearby town. Her clues resulted in the murderer's arrest. The story was later written up in the *National Enquirer*.

At first she was thrilled at her discovery of being psychic. But her joy began to change as frightening things happened to her. Rest became more and more elusive as nightmares invaded her sleep. Grotesque, leering faces unexpectedly appeared when she open-ed closet doors or entered other rooms. Coming along a hallway, she would suddenly smash into an invisi-ble wall.

Tormented, she sought help from other psychics who, on arriving at her home, declared they could hardly move around in the living room because of the density of the presence of evil spirits.

It was at this point of desperation, with no apparent help to be found, that her story was printed in the newspaper.

Roy and I heard the story from several people in our church after we returned from a three-day cruise—a birthday present from the church to their pastor.

"We phoned and told them Jesus was the answer," one church member told me.

"We told them they needed deliverance in the name of Jesus," another said.

In response to calls and letters from our church members, the young woman decided to visit us. I talk-ed with her an hour.

As we spoke, her body shook and twitched, and her teeth chattered so violently she had difficulty speak-ing. I explained that James 2:19 says that demons believe there is a God and tremble.

"Satan has power, but Jesus has *all* power," I said. "We call our heavenly Father 'the Almighty' and believe Him to be just that. If you want to yield your life to Jesus and renounce all desire and contact with psychic power, then the battle is the Lord's. And He's always the winner. But the decision is completely yours. I won't force you to do anything."

The young woman chose to commit her life to Jesus. "I'm still afraid, though," she said.

However, armed with Scripture verses to encourage her faith and defeat her fear, she left.

Several days later a group from church drove to her house. We were fortified by prayer and fasting and God's Word and were not afraid. We knew the presence of the Holy Spirit was within us.

None of us claimed to be exorcists. In fact, three of us were housewives; the other two, ministers.

After a brief conversation, the born-again but still psychic woman said, "I see a masked man with a raised hatchet standing behind one of the ladies." She was amazed that we were seemingly undisturbed.

I had dealt many times with demon-possessed people but never before with a demon-possessed house. We walked through each room, commanding every evil spirit to leave in the name of Jesus.

Finally, we returned to the living room to work with the young mother. She was in a trance, rocking and cackling like a storybook witch.

But as occult spirits were commanded to come out of her, they did—some with a loud noise.

When we were done, we could see an expression of joy light up her face. She had peace. She was free.

In January of the following year the newspaper ran another story about the house and family. This time it had a happy ending.

22

A Cure for Cancer

When I picked up the ringing phone, I immediately recognized Pat's voice on the other end. She was a friend who lived in another city. But today's unexpected call was not to be just a friendly chat.

"Pauline, I'm scared!" Pat blurted out desperately. "The doctors here in the hospital have taken some tests. They've discovered cell abnormalities, and they are very concerned. When I ask if it is cancer, they shake their heads and say, 'We are hoping not.' "

Pat began to sob. "I think I'm going to die . . . . All of my immediate family have died of cancer at an early age — I'm the only one left."

She struggled for emotional control and then asked me, "Surely God wouldn't give me two tiny babies and then let me die and leave them, would He?"

"Surely he wouldn't," I echoed. Pat was a fine Christian. She had worked at our church, and after marrying a wonderful man, they had moved to another city.

"I try to find Scriptures on healing that I heard at your church," she continued, "but I can't even find *one*."

I felt this precious woman's plight and began to console her. "Pat, not very long ago I went through some deep waters and couldn't even pray for myself. All I could do was weep and say, 'Lord, lay me on somebody's heart. Have them intercede on my behalf.' I discovered that right at those times first one, then another, would be burdened for me.

"Pat, the Lord wants to meet your need even if you don't know where the answers are."

Then I felt the Spirit impress me to give her some advice. "As you lie on your back in that hospital room, I want you to say, 'Underneath are the Everlasting Arms — I'm lying in God's arms.' Next, adamantly refuse the fear. When it wants to flood over you, say, 'God gave Jesus a name above every name, a name even greater than *cancer*. Therefore, I am not afraid of cancer because of Jesus.' Finally, let your husband, your friend Carol, and I do the praying for you at this time."

Pat thanked me. "I feel more peaceful now," she said.

Before our conversation ended, Roy and I prayed for her.

The next day I called her to see how she was doing.

"Just one area has the doctors worried," Pat said. "They have cautioned me. All other tests are negative."

"Doctors are wonderful," I told her, "however, they do not know everything. So our faith continues after the doctors have put a 'period.' "

At 7:15 the next morning I again called to pray and encourage her as she took further tests. I quoted Psalm 56:11, "In God have I put my trust: I will not be afraid what man can do unto me." Then I said,

"Hold on to that verse."

At 10 a.m. Pat called me back. "Pauline, there's no cancer! The doctors are baffled — just like you prayed they would be. I just have some swelling either in the gall bladder or the pancreas. I'm so thrilled."

So was I. I breathed a sigh of relief and praise. Pat's friend Carol had stayed awake all the previous night, concerned and prayerful. I knew she would rejoice with us.

Through my experiences with people such as Pat, I have found some general principles that I apply in life's crisis times.

The first thing I do is rebuke Satan. I come against him with the blood of the Lamb, the sword of the Spirit (which is the Bible), the name of Jesus, and the power of the Holy Spirit. These four weapons are available to us through Jesus. He paid the price that we might fight the battle and have victory through these means.

Another weapon I use against Satan is the "word" of our "testimony" (Rev. 12:11). Being able to use this weapon is solely up to me. I have to keep my life pure and walk in submission to the King of kings so that Satan will recognize whose child I am. Then I can speak as one of the sons and daughters of the most high God and with the authority that He has given.

I also quote John 16:23, "Whatsoever ye shall ask the Father in my name, he will give it you." Then I say, "Father, according to Your Word, I ask in Jesus' name." Then I place my petition before Him.

I also repeat Mark 11:23, "Whosoever shall say unto this mountain, Be thou removed, and be thou cast into the sea; and shall not doubt in his heart, but shall believe that those things which he saith shall come to pass; he shall have whatsoever he saith." I say out loud, "I believe that what I *say* shall come to pass."

In all of these actions I keep my mind centered on God's love, just as I had told Pat to do. First Corinthians 10:13 declares, "There hath no temptation taken you but such as is common to man: but God is faithful, who will not suffer you to be tempted above that ye are able; but will with the temptation also make a way to escape, that ye may be able to bear it."

Beyond all my ways and attempts to do and say the right things, I have to remember that a faithful, loving God is always with me. And when I don't have all the answers, I know that He does.

He met Pat's need and has met so many of mine. As we look to Him instead of the problems around us, our loving Father meets our needs.

23

Speaking against Insecurity

I didn't know what to do with them. I didn't know what to say. I had no answers, and I didn't know how to help.

Four pairs of eyes looked to me to come up with a solution. A weary, defeated mother and three frightened children — an 18-year-old son, a 15-year-old daughter, and a ten-year-old boy.

Susan had come to me two years before, desperately in need of spiritual help. Her husband had found another woman and wanted a divorce.

In her late 30s, Susan had always been controlled by somebody. First it was her parents and then her husband. She found it impossible to make a decision. Even simple decisions such as whether to go to McDonald's or Burger King for a hamburger defeated her. She would go home without one.

Compounding her problems was the knowledge

that her husband was involved with the occult, using it in his business deals and his personal life.

She had been involved in the occult a little herself. In the times we had met together in the past she was unable to follow simple spiritual instructions or even concentrate on our conversations.

Now, here she was again, under satanic attack. Her eyes were glazed, and she seemed to be in a stupor. Her thoughts were rambling, and her speech was slurred.

I asked her gently if she had taken any drugs or been drinking. She hadn't been, but she told me how difficult it was to think — or to act.

Over and over again she said, "I am not a fit mother. The children must go to their father. They don't want to go, but he wants to have them. I just cannot cope. I'm losing my mind."

We were all standing at the front of the church building. I put my arms around her and tried to comfort her. "Oh, Susan," I said, "I didn't know things were this bad. There's got to be an answer. You're going to make it."

She began to moan. I knew she and the children expected me to come up with an answer. But I didn't have one.

I quickly began sending up silent prayers. "Holy Spirit, You must help me. I don't know what to say or what to do. She is so emotionally drained and depressed she is almost helpless. You know what needs to be said. Please give me the words."

I felt her husband's involvement with the occult (he had often practiced witchcraft) was contributing to her problems. So I took authority over any satanic harassment.

Then God reminded me of an incident that had taken place about six months earlier.

At the end of a church service Susan had suffered a heart attack. For minutes she was in severe pain.

Someone phoned an ambulance while others gathered around and prayed for her. Finally, a handful of us stayed with her while she rested on a pew.

The ambulance arrived, and the men from the rescue squad ran in. Susan hadn't realized they were coming, and when she saw them, she began to protest. Firmly but quietly she said, "I am not going to the hospital. I've been prayed for, and I'm healed."

Her son immediately spoke up. "Mother, I'm the man of the house now. I sent for the ambulance. I'm concerned about you. You must go to the hospital."

"Thank you, son," she replied, "but I'm not going to the hospital."

The paramedics tried to get her on the stretcher. Everyone began to express their opinions. Some were adamant that she should go to the hospital. Others agreed with her. Then they appealed to me.

"I think it is important that Susan make the decision and then that we stand with her and back her up, whichever she decides," I said. "Personally, I feel I cannot be responsible to choose for her. Let her make the choice."

Susan chose to go home. I was elated, not just by her choice, but by the quiet, firm strength she exhibited.

And she was healed. Her doctor certified that she had had a heart attack, but she had no more problems. I told her then how proud I was that she had made a decision and was so calm and clearheaded.

So now the Holy Spirit reminded me of that incident.

"Susan," I said, "I want you to remember that time several months ago when you had a heart attack in church. Remember how adamant you were in refusing to go to the hospital? How firm you were with your son? How firmly you opposed those who tried to get you on a stretcher and how stubbornly insistent you were that you were healed? You even said, 'I am 39 years old, a grown woman. I can make my own decisions." With the Holy Spirit's help, let that conquering spirit rise again. Make definite decisions right now and voice them."

In a small voice she began. "I am a capable mother . . . . I can look after these children. I can cope with life. I shall not lose my mind."

Her voice grew louder and more indignant. "My children will be raised by me in a Christian home, not in the ungodly atmosphere of their father and his new wife. All of us are under the protection of the blood of Jesus. Satan has no power over us.

"We will live healthy, happy, well-adjusted lives. God will provide for us in every area of our lives — spirit, soul, and body. These things I decree in Jesus' mighty name."

Just words? No. They were decision-making words. She made a bold confession of faith in the middle of her trials. As she spoke spiritual truth, her insecurities crumbled.

Satan was defeated in Susan's life when she trusted God's security.

24

Transformed by God's Power

It was 3 a.m. and Big Jim was drunk again. He was in his 30s, living his own wild life, half a continent away from his mother.

When Big Jim was drunk, he often called home. He wanted his mother to pray for him. Tonight he called again but this time had a different request.

"Mama, I met this girl Linda at a bar. We've been talking. She keeps having to get surgery on her feet. The growths keep coming back," he said, getting his mother's sleepy attention.

"She has to have surgery again soon and she's scared. Real scared. I said you'd pray for her, mama. You will, won't you?" Jim blurted out.

"Yes, Jim, I will. But you listen to me. If you really want to help this girl, take her to a Bible-believing church this Sunday. Promise me."

"O.K., mama. Will do."

The following Sunday Jim dropped Linda off at our church and promised to pick her up after the service was over.

"Aren't you coming in, too?" Linda asked.

"No," Jim responded. "I was reared in a church like that. I know all about it." He didn't admit that he was afraid to go in — afraid that his mother's prayers, the familiar hymns, and the preaching might get to him.

The happy faces, spontaneous worship, and presence of the Holy Spirit awed Linda. Delight and conviction alternately overwhelmed her. She wanted to be a part of what she saw. She grabbed her crutches (used temporarily because of her foot condition) and hobbled down the aisle to accept Jesus into her heart.

She overflowed with happiness when Jim picked her up.

"I can't wait to tell you what happened to me!" she exclaimed, lighting a cigarette. "Jesus is in my heart. I'm so happy I'm afraid I'll burst."

Jim was angry. He didn't profess to be a Christian, but he knew what one was like. And Christians didn't smoke!

They argued as Jim drove her home. Linda invited him in for a drink; he exploded again when she poured herself one, too.

She knew nothing about living a Christian life but was convinced Jesus lived in her. He knew all about the Christian life, and Christians were not supposed to drink or smoke.

Despite their quarrels, Big Jim and Linda fell in love and were married. Shortly thereafter she underwent the foot operation. But the scars didn't heal, and other tumors reappeared.

One night, Jim and Linda invited Roy and me to dinner. We knew very little about them except that we heard she was a radiant Christian and he was a backslider. They had both decided to ask the preacher whether Linda was a Christian, and they explained the situation to us.

"Jim, why don't you stop playing Linda's conscience and get concerned about yourself?" my husband asked. "And, Linda, why don't you ask Jesus if these things are really pleasing to Him?"

This appeared to please both, and things began to happen. One evening Linda realized she needed deliverance from the occult in which she had been actively, but innocently, involved: Ouija boards, séances, palm reading — and foot reading.

As we prayed, she took off her shoes. All the tumors had disappeared; all the scars were healed.

After Christmas, she told me, "I gave Jesus a Christmas present. It wasn't easy after all these years, but I gave Jesus the smoking and the drinking. I know I'm a better witness for Him without them."

And Big Jim? He surrendered his life in his office one day and was instantly baptized in the Holy Spirit. For hours he was so drunk on "New Wine" he couldn't drive home.

And he never wanted old wine after that.

25

The Christian Domino Effect

It was during the latter half of World War II. Our home had been blitzed, our school bombed to the ground, and our church completely wiped out. Finally, after meeting in homes and an unused store, our church had been rebuilt.

Living in the outskirts of London, we had seen and experienced heartache and sorrow. Every day brought death and destruction. Many nights we remained fully clothed, ready for emergencies (ours or someone else's).

One rainy, blustery winter evening, we held a street meeting before the Tuesday prayer meeting. We had a particularly hard time on the street corner that evening. Among the distractions was a dirty and unkempt teenage girl, who tried to ride her bike in and out of the circle, splashing mud up the backs of our legs.

111

My mother suddenly spoke to the girl.

"Would you do something for me?" she asked. "Be a sweetheart and hold this hymnbook while I play the accordion."

The girl gave a cocky little smirk but obliged. Inside, Sharon admitted later, she wanted to cry. This lady spoke with so much love.

She was one of 17 children; her parents had never married. Her mother was sick in bed in a big, stately house nearby, among other nice homes. Her family had been placed there by the government after bombs had destroyed their home. And the neighbors resented them.

When the street meeting ended, Sharon didn't want to leave. "I want to go to church with you," she insisted. My mother suggested she wait until Sunday (our prayer meetings were prayer only and lasted two or three hours), but the girl persisted.

As we all walked to church, I prayed, "Please, Lord, don't let the Power fall. Don't let anyone give an utterance in tongues tonight."

I think God forgave me. He also ignored me.

Sharon tugged at my mother's sleeve during the prayer meeting and whispered, "I want to be like you." Mom understood, but did Sharon? Mom led her to the Lord and left it with Him.

She was at the next service, but we didn't recognize her. Sparkling clean, new clothes, shining hair, sweet-smelling — God had performed a miracle inside and out.

"Would you visit my sister in the hospital? She's dying," Sharon requested. The sister already had one little boy afflicted by syphilis, and she was dying after a botched-up abortion. She wept with joy as she accepted Jesus — and died rejoicing in Him.

Sharon's next request — visiting her mother — was somehow harder. The woman had been a madam of a brothel. My mother was always compassionate, bringing home waifs and working with the poor; but the fat, smelly, toothless woman revolted her.

"Tell her about Me," God spoke to my mother's heart.

"Yes, Lord, of course."

"Now put your arms around her and kiss her."

"I don't think I can! Help me!" But she did, and the woman broke into uncontrollable sobbing. She accepted Jesus, was healed, and led the father of her 17 children to the Lord. The children still at home accepted Jesus, too.

The whole family was baptized a short time later. They cleaned, painted, and wallpapered their home; scrubbed the children; and dressed them in clean clothes.

Many years have passed, and I am not sure where many of them are. But Sharon has been richly blessed. Now a gentle, refined lady, she is married to a fine man and has a lovely home. She loves to reminisce about what Jesus did in their lives more than 30 years ago.

And wherever the others are, I'm sure they remember the transformation that took place in their hearts and home.

26

Conquering the Shadow of Death

The Ilniskys enjoyed their visit at their daughter's home, but it was getting late. They had to leave.

The rain poured down as the old couple hurried to their car. They were in their 70s and moved as fast as they could to the car's dry safeness.

Mr. Ilnisky started the car and headed home. He had taken this route many times. The heavy rain and poor visibility shouldn't be too much of a problem.

He turned his car up the ramp of the interstate highway. This was the fastest way home. As he accelerated, something seemed wrong. Several sets of headlights were bearing down on him.

Before he could react, he and his wife were smashed into unconsciousness. They had been hit by another car head-on. Mr. Ilnisky had turned up an exit ramp instead of an entrance ramp to the highway.

Their car was so mangled that a state trooper who reported the accident could not tell what make or model it was.

Although the passengers in the other car escaped serious injury, the Ilniskys were critically injured. They were rushed to the hospital emergency room.

Family members were quickly notified of the tragedy and hurried to the hospital. Bill and Esther Ilnisky, missionaries in Lebanon, immediately flew to the States to be with their parents.

My husband also hurried to the hospital. As their pastor, he wanted to see if he could help. When he arrived, the doctor took him aside. "Don't let the family see their parents until the faces are bandaged," he said. Then he described some of the injuries. Mrs. Ilnisky looked as if someone had smashed every bone in her face with a sledge hammer, the doctor said. Her head was swollen and shaped like a football. Her eyes were where her mouth should be.

"I don't see any hope for either of them," the doctor continued. "Notify the family that they're dying."

Word quickly spread about the Ilniskys' accident. Members of our church where they had been active reacted to the news in one of two ways.

One group took the attitude that the Ilniskys had been wonderful faithful servants of God all their lives and this was finally God's time to "take them home." Besides, the Ilniskys had already lived out their biblical threescore and ten years, this group said.

Another group believed, however, that it was not God's will for His children to die in such a hideous accident. This group referred to John 10:10 and said, "Satan comes to steal, kill, and destroy. Surely this is the work of the enemy. We must do battle with him."

This group began to pray in church prayer meetings and home prayer groups, as couples and as individuals.

At the end of a midweek service, my husband

asked the whole church to pray.

We started the prayer by praising God, thanking Him that through Jesus healing power was available for this wonderful couple and that by Christ's stripes they were healed.

But that wasn't all. We also rebuked Satan and bound the spirits of coma, trauma, death, unconsciousness, injury, and accident in the name of Jesus.

Some of the people were surprised to hear this type of prayer. But when Jesus had trouble with the devil, He didn't fall on His knees and plead with God to help. Rather, He told the devil, "Get hence," or "Get thee behind Me."

At the same time we were praying, Mrs. Ilnisky's heart stopped beating. The doctor pronounced her dead.

But then her heart began beating again, and her body became warm and supple. The doctor was shocked.

The doctor said later he had proclaimed many patients dead and that he knew a dead body when he saw one. Mrs. Ilnisky had been dead.

She remembers leaving her body and looking down at her hideous, mangled face.

About the same time, Mr. Ilnisky was taken to surgery for major internal repair, including mending a torn bladder. When the doctors began surgery, they discovered the "Great Physician" had already performed the healing with no stitches necessary.

The Ilniskys became known around the hospital as the "miracle couple."

Several years have passed, and the Ilniskys are completely healed and enjoy Divine health to its fullest. They came through the valley of the shadow of death.

27

A Baby
Is Set Free

"I don't know what I'm going to do," Jennie
said, looking at me through bloodshot eyes. "I've got
to get some rest."

"What's wrong?" I quickly asked.

"It's Craig," the young mother responded. "He's six
months old, and ever since he was born, we have not
had more than two hours of sleep at night. He
screams constantly."

Jennie told me he acted as though he were in great
pain, holding and pulling his ears. Every few days he
was at the doctor's office. The doctor was completely baffled with him and had called other doctors in
on the case. They had run tubes down his ears but
could find nothing.

Now Jennie didn't have the money to keep going
to the doctor, or for the tests, or the medication.

Jennie told me another problem had also arisen.

As a new Christian, she was anxious to get all the teaching she could, but when she attended church, at the beginning of every sermon, she was sent for by the nursery staff. Not only could they not quiet Craig, but he had all the others screaming too. They suggested that she look after him in a room by herself. Of course, she might just as well stay home.

We sat in silence for a few moments. Then I said, "Jennie, you once mentioned spiritualism. Tell me more about your contacts with the psychic medium."

She told me that a few months before Craig was born and before she became a Christian, she had heard of a group of psychics not too far from where we live who could tell about the past, including some things of which the person might not even be aware; predict the future; and offer help in any problem areas of life.

Because quotations of Jesus and parts of the Bible were used, along with the singing of certain hymns and the offering of prayers, visiting the psychics seemed very beautiful and very right. These people really seemed to have a powerful God who worked on their behalf and was the answer to all of life's problems, Jennie said.

"I went twice and had what's called 'readings.' It was such an exciting experience and gave me a sense of well-being," she said.

"However, on my third visit, I suddenly felt an icy chill come over me. I got terribly afraid, and that night I was scared to sleep without a light — and still am. Also I have the feeling that someone is always lurking in the shadows and looking at me."

"Jennie," I said, "you have been involved in the occult, and no matter how innocently you were drawn into these things, nor with what genuine desires you were seeking for the supernatural, you were contacting the wrong source of power. And you *have* made contact."

Jennie and I prayed together. She asked God's forgiveness and renounced all involvement with the occult. We commanded all fear to leave and every connection with the occult powers to be gone.

Soon Jennie laughed and cried with joy, knowing that she was completely free.

I told her to bring Craig into the prayer room the next time she came to church, and we would pray for him.

The following night she brought him, a darling, handsome little fellow. He sat on the floor at one end of the room, playing with his mother's bracelets.

A little unsure of how to deal with the baby's problem and not wanting to frighten him, I stood at the other end of the room and quietly but firmly demanded that any occult spirit from the psychic, any spirit causing pain, and any restless spirit of insomnia leave in Jesus' name.

He suddenly burst into tears and just as quickly stopped crying. Next he held his ears and cried as if in pain, then ceased. He also "threw-up" his bottle. Jennie and I looked at each other and shrugged a little questioningly.

"I guess time will tell if we were on target with our prayers, Jennie," I said. "Phone me sometime."

The next morning she phoned. "Craig was so happy as I drove him home. He dropped off to sleep before I got there. He stayed asleep as I carried him in and even while I undressed him, changed him, and dressed him for bed. 'We'll have our first good night tonight,' I said to my unbelieving husband. 'Craig was prayed for.' "

That night Craig slept nine and one-half hours without stirring.

Several years have now passed, and Jennie recently told me that when Craig returned to the church nursery, he gained the reputation from nursery workers as "the best youngun here."

28

Great Miracles — Even in Little Things

I sat at the table, pondering my assignment for a magazine article. I was to write something on the theme, "Don't Limit God."

Immediately I thought of His attributes. He is limitless in power, love, and holiness. I recalled some of the miracles I had seen God perform — incurable diseases healed, tormented minds set free, marriages restored, parents and children reconciled.

I glanced up from my work as my daughter Elizabeth entered the room. "What is the greatest miracle you've experienced in our famliy?" I asked on impulse.

"Tiny," she replied without hesitation.

I remembered Tiny's miracle well. It was an example to me that God is concerned about "little" as well as "big" things.

I have met many people who have a false idea about

God. They think He is so big and impersonal that He couldn't be involved in the small things in our lives.

Of course, testimonies of God's great miracles are exciting. Yet, when God answers little prayers, I think it thrills me even more. His minute attention to every little detail of our lives is breathtaking.

When our son, Charles, was about four years old, he decided to take his little green turtle, about the size of a half dollar, for a walk in the grass. In a short while, he ran into the house, saying, "Mommy, please come and help me. Tid-bit went through the chain-link fence."

We searched and searched in vain. That night he said, "Let's pray that we find him."

Several days later, my next-door neighbor asked if I was afraid to pick up little crawly green turtles. The neighbor next to her had opened her front door to find the tiny creature on her doorstep.

On another occasion, one of our girls had several guinea pigs. She brought one to show me. "Look, mom. He only has one eye, poor fellow." Sure enough, he had one brown eye and the other was completely white.

"Pray for him, mom, for a miracle."

I gently stroked the little animal's head. "Why don't you pray for him, darling? He's your pet."

Actually, I couldn't pray. I just did not have the faith. And I hated to see her disappointed when prayer was not answered.

As I drove up the driveway with groceries the next day, my daughter met me with a guinea pig cupped in her hands. "Look at his eye!" she said. "It's a miracle."

I looked at the guinea pig and its two brown eyes. Then I chuckled as I thought I caught on to her teasing ways. "Aw, come on," I laughed, "you switched guinea pigs on me, didn't you?"

"Oh, no," she replied, acting stunned that I would

think such a thing. "This is the one I showed you yesterday. His blind eye is healed. I prayed for him last night."

And then there was Tiny's miracle. His full name is Tiny-wee Harthern, a very big name for a toy Pomeranian not much larger than a squirrel.

Our family was at church, cooperating with Christians all over the nation of every race and creed in a day of prayer and fasting for our nation. It seemed such a day of victory that toward the conclusion of the prayer meeting the thought occurred to me, "Satan must be in a fury tonight." I asked the Lord to protect all of us at the prayer meeting — our husbands, wives, children, and our cars — as we traveled home.

When our family arrived home, Tiny ran out to greet us, barking furiously. He has an awfully loud bark for such a little dog, and I quickly gathered him up so the neighbors would not be disturbed.

He wriggled in my hands, and one little paw became entangled in my necklace. I tried to free him, and he slipped from my grasp, falling hard to the ground.

I picked up his limp body and began to pace the floor, saying, "In the name of Jesus." The three girls joined in. Suddenly his body stiffened and his heart, which had felt like a watch ticking against my hand, ceased to beat.

Three years earlier, when our little poodle was killed by a car, we had not prayed. We simply buried him. But this seemed an obvious satanic attack against our little dog. We believed it as such and after 30 minutes of claiming, rebuking, and praising, we saw Tiny take an enormous breath. Then his heart began beating. Although it was not until the following morning that he was able to stand, he soon regained his complete health.

God had a great answer for a seemingly unimportant thing. I'm sure He does attend the funeral of a sparrow.

And no miracle is too big or small for Him. He meets all His children's needs.

29

What You Say Can Help or Hurt You

It was a sad story and my heart went out to her. At the age of 20 she had received shock treatment. Now, 30 years later, she was still under psychiatric care. Her present physician had been her psychiatrist for 14 years.

She talked with real anguish of soul. She was a dedicated Christian devoted to her fine husband and four lovely children, yet she was unable to cope with the emotional turmoil within.

She was plagued continuously with tormenting questions: "Am I normal? Am I doomed to hell? What will happen to my husband and children?"

She was continually questioning and analyzing, never free from anxiety — unable to sleep at night because of her relentless, driving, tormenting thoughts; unable to work at the simplest of household chores during the day; exhausted, yet unable to be still.

My heart went out to her. I longed more than anything to be able to help her.

However, as I listened patiently, silently to her that morning, she kept repeating one line of thought every so often. "Oh, what am I going to do? I *know* no one can help me. I *know* I'm going to finish up in the mental ward of the hospital.

"Oh, please, please, will you help me?" she implored. "Please, will you pray for me? I beg of you, help me. Oh, I know no one can help me; I know I'll finish up in psychiatric care. Shall I throw away my pills? Do you want me to stop going to see the psychiatrist? Will you pray for me? Can you do something?"

As gently as I could, I said, "No. I cannot pray for you — yet."

"Why not, oh, why not? I'm desperate. Don't you want to help me. What am I going to do?"

I said, "To pray for you now would be to compound your problems. You are confessing that no one can help you, that you are on your way to a mental institution.

"If you will confess the positive Word of God, I'll be happy to help you. I'll give you three pages of faith-building Scriptures. If you'll start confessing those, I'll stay with you until you get complete victory."

She was hurt. A look of disappointment and hopelessness came across her face. I tried to explain to her: "It isn't that God isn't the answer. He is. But He has given us weapons with which to fight the enemy.

"First there is Jesus' name," I told her. "Mark 16:17 says, 'In my name ye shall cast out devils.'

"Next, there is the Word of God. Jesus used this against Satan.

"Third, we have the power of the Holy Ghost. The Greek word for *power* is *dunamis;* our word *dynamite* is derived from the same word.

"Fourth, there is the blood of the Lamb. Revelation 12:11 says, 'They overcame the devil by the blood of the Lamb, and by the word of their testimony.'

"The last weapon, 'the word of their testimony,' is entirely up to us. The words we speak can help defeat the devil. To confess otherwise brings glory and power to Satan and cancels out the effectiveness of prayer."

I reminded her of the Scriptures, "Death and life are in the power of the tongue" (Prov. 18:21), "By thy words thou shalt be condemned" (Matt. 12:37), and "For as he thinketh in his heart so is he" (Prov. 23:7). Then, armed with other Scriptures, she left.

But she did not look at them, and the wonderful words of God were no more help to her than a bottle of tonic, unopened and left in the cupboard.

One day the psychiatrist phoned my home. He happened to be a Christian. "Mrs. Harthern, I understand that you are counseling one of my patients.

"Mrs. Harthern, no one can help her; but if you do help her, you'll make a believer in deliverance out of me."

Then the dark and tragic day which she had been confessing came to pass. Strapped down, crying, begging, pleading and screaming, she was taken to psychiatric care.

While I and others continued to pray for her, she remained in the hospital. In her torment and desperation she thought, "Nothing's worked. Why don't I at least try the Word of God.

" 'Greater is He that is in me, than he that is in the world;' 'God hath not given us the Spirit of fear, but of power and of love and of a sound mind;' 'If God be for me, who can be against me?' " she repeated.

Shortly after, she improved and was released. After that, her phone calls to me were made in faith instead of doubt and hopelessness. She would begin each conversation with, "I am praising God for my salvation, my healing, and my deliverance."

After about three weeks of pronouncing her faith in Jesus the Deliverer, and after quoting the Word, she met with several of us for prayer. We commanded every tormenting spirit to leave her mind. At times a spirit would protest or object or argue.

But that day this lovely woman was set free — totally — after many years of torment.

She is now working at a good job as well as looking after her family and home. She is a radiant Christian, and as the Bible says, she is "a joyful mother of children."

And the psychiatrist? He spoke the truth. He now prays deliverance for some of his patients.

30

Raining on the Just

During a period when my husband had been teaching on stewardship of such things as time, talents, and money, he invited a number of people to testify concerning God's promise in Malachi 3:10: "Bring ye all the tithes into the storehouse, that there may be meat in mine house, and prove me now herewith, saith the Lord of hosts, if I will not open you the windows of heaven, and pour you out a blessing, that there shall not be room enough to receive it."

It was thrilling to hear of God's blessing being poured out of the open windows of heaven upon those who honored Him in obedience to His command concerning tithes and offerings.

But there was one man who had quite a different story.

Larry McCown, a rice farmer and a relatively new convert, stood and said, "I haven't been a Christian

131

very long, but I want to be faithful to the Lord no matter what happens in my life. I've been giving my tithes and offerings to Him, and God has drawn our family closer together.

"Well, last week we had a pretty bad storm," Larry continued, his voice starting to break with emotion. "The rain knocked the matured rice off the plants. My whole crop was ruined. We've lost everything. I don't know how we're going to get through this year."

He told us he had obtained a loan to begin with in order to purchase and plant the rice seed. The harvest would have given him enough money to live on after repaying the loan.

"I want to tell you," Larry concluded, "I love Jesus Christ, and I'm still going to live for Him." Many of us found ourselves weeping with him as he sat down.

Shortly after that, our family moved from the area and lost contact with Larry and his family. During the next year I frequently wondered about them and prayed for them.

One year passed, and my son went back to Texas for a visit. While he was there, Larry again stood up in church, telling what was happening in his life.

"We just had another bad storm," Larry began. "When the rains came, I cried out, 'Oh, God, not again, not again. I can't believe this.'

"When I got to my fields, they were dry. Rain was falling on the fields all around me but not on mine. I actually stood at the edge of my property and put out my hand and felt the rain that was falling on a neighbor's field.

"All the rice farmers around me have ruined crops. Their rice is rotting in the fields. But not a drop of water hit my rice. I have the largest crop I've ever had."

Larry became the talk of Beaumont, Texas. His crop was the only one in the entire area not ruined.

He had proven God, not allowing circumstances to diminish his faith. The result was that he was blessed financially and became a testimony to the entire community of God's faithfulness to those who honor His Word.

31

By Whose Stripes
I Am Healed

As Roy drove me home from the hospital that morning, my heart kept ringing with the thought, "Reprieved. Reprieved."

I had entered the hospital for surgery for a growth about which two doctors were quite concerned. They urged me not to procrastinate. Although I, too, was anxious, I was hoping for a miracle.

The surgery had been scheduled early that Tuesday morning but was postponed for two weeks because my throat had become sore from the air conditioner blowing on me the previous night.

Two weeks! Now, I thought, if someone, somewhere will lay hands on me who has the gifts of healing, the gift of faith, or the working of miracles, then I will not need surgery.

This had happened ten years before when Oral Roberts laid hands on me during an Atlanta tent revival. I felt a sort of "whoosh," and I was healed. He knew it; I knew it; we all knew it.

The words of Peter filtered through my mind now, "By whose stripes ye were healed" (1 Pet. 2:24).

"Oh, yes, Lord, that will be my testimony if I can just feel the 'whoosh' again," I quietly told Him.

"By whose stripes ye were healed." My husband had preached on that. But what about the pain? What if it were cancer? What about the rapid growth from lemon-size to tangerine-size?

Did God's Word mean it was done? Was I supposed to ignore symptoms? Did it mean to look back to Calvary's finished work rather than to a healing experience in the future?

I remembered the prophecy concerning Jesus in Isaiah 53:4-5, "Surely he hath borne our griefs, and carried our sorrows: yet we did esteem him stricken, smitten of God, and afflicted. But he was wounded for our transgressions, he was bruised for our iniquities: the chastisement of our peace was upon Him; and with His stripes we are healed."

Jesus bore my griefs and my sorrows. I knew the original Hebrew says that "griefs" (choili) means "pains," and "sorrows" (makob) means "sicknesses."

I'd trusted Him for sins, but if He also bore my sicknesses, then this growth did not belong to me. Right there I made a decision. It was made almost as an experiment. I believe it could be said that doubt was the underlying ingredient.

"By whose stripes ye *were* healed." I repeated the verse out loud literally hundreds of times daily — sometimes questioningly, sometimes with determination. Sometimes I would say it absentmindedly while peeling potatoes, washing diapers, waxing furniture. I'd say it on going to bed, or arising — "By whose stripes ye were healed."

It was like a spiritual seesaw at first. "By whose stripes ye were healed."

What if it's cancer? "By whose stripes . . ."

But I'm in pain; the growth's larger; I'm scared. "By whose stripes *I am healed!*"

Doubt changed to hope. Then about eight days later, it really took hold. Hope became faith. To the delight of our four babies, I danced around, saying, "I'm healed. I'm healed."

It had become a deep unshakable fact. God had said it. It was so.

I phoned my husband at the church. I simply said, "Roy, I'm healed."

"Great!" he rejoiced. "Has the growth gone?"

"No."

"The pain's gone?"

"No."

"Well . . ."

"Well, I *know* I'm healed."

Two days later, the church bulletin came in the mail. My husband, by whose teaching on claiming God's Word I had obtained healing, had written, "Pray for my wife. She is entering the hospital for surgery on Monday."

I called him again. I said, "Roy Harthern, your bulletin is wrong. I am healed and will not have surgery."

On Monday afternoon I had my bag packed to go to the hospital. On the way we stopped by my doctor's office to check to see that I had no sore throat.

My pain was there; the growth, now the size of an orange, was still there. But I knew somehow surgery would not be necessary.

The doctor sat me on his table and began probing. He frowned and probed again. He looked at his papers on my case and said, "Am I on the wrong side? I can't find any growth."

He called in two specialists from the medical center who also read my medical history, asked questions, probed around, and finally concluded, "There is nothing there on which to operate."

As much as I enjoy instantaneous healing, relying on God's Word did more to increase my faith than any other experience.

32

Redeemed

We were so excited. We could hardly wait for the car to stop so we could get to the little six-month-old puppy in it. We all wanted to love him and care for him and let him know that he would never be mistreated again.

He would have food and fresh water, we would be his family, and he would never be frightened anymore.

But we were totally unprepared for what took place. Fighting, snarling, snapping, and biting, he soon let us know he didn't want us near him; in fact, he wanted nothing to do with us.

The kind lady who had rescued him finally dragged him into the house on a long rope, while he stubbornly sat on his haunches, yipping, growling, snapping, and protesting — fighting every inch of the way.

Then she was gone, and we were left with a frantic, frenzied animal that was trying to escape from us.

What a pitiable sight he was. His poodle coat had never been trimmed. It was a solid mass of knots, snarls, and tangles. Even so, his bones looked in places as though they were ready to poke through his flesh, which was full of sores and scabs. And, oh!, how bad he smelled.

Five months before this he had been an adorable baby puppy, friendly but shy, mischievous but gentle. He was sold along with his brothers and sisters to what we thought were good homes.

We heard nothing more of him until almost five months later when the phone rang and a voice on the other end said, "Are you Mrs. Harthern?"

"Yes, I am."

"Did you sell a puppy to Mrs. Blane several months ago?"

"Yes, I did. Why?"

"I am a neighbor and a nurse. Mrs. Blane is a drug addict. I have never seen an animal more neglected or mistreated than that puppy. He is left for days at a time without food in the garage. Other neighbors have heard him crying and whimpering. One day I found him in the garbage can with a cat. The lid was on the can. I have just found him in the garage under a heavy bookcase which had toppled on top of him. He is still alive. Do you think you could call the authorities?"

I phoned Mrs. Blane. I simply stated that I wanted my dog back. She said I couldn't have him back because he was her dog and was very valuable. I offered to buy him back for what I sold him to her. She said no, because he was worth twice that much.

I said, "I want you to know that I am buying that dog back or going to the humane society with a complaint. Which do you prefer? For I am having him back."

We sat on the floor now, gently, soothingly speaking to the shivering, whimpering animal that seemed to be pressing his quivering body into the very walls which held him prisoner.

"We love you."

"Don't be afraid anymore."

Minutes passed; hours passed; the frightened eyes gazed back at us. Tremblingly, the little creature inched out of the corner. Uncertainly he crept toward us, and finally our patience was rewarded with a feeble lick on our outstretched hand.

He's our dog now, and we continue to care for him. Loving, fiercely loyal, he's always underfoot, even wanting to be cuddled. He doesn't look the same.

He has been redeemed.

Books and Tapes
From Roy Harthern Ministries

	donation price	quantity	total donation
NEW BOOKLETS			
Speaking Creative Words	$ 2.25	× _____	= _____
From Tragedy to Triumph	$ 2.25	× _____	= _____
The Blessings of Forgiving	$ 2.25	× _____	= _____
PAULINE'S NEW DELUXE HARDBACK			
Miracles from My Diary	$ 9.50	× _____	= _____
CASSETTE TEACHING TAPES			
Spiritual Warfare			
(3 tapes by Roy Harthern)	$15.00	× _____	= _____
How to Find the Will of God			
(3 tapes by Pauline Harthern)	$15.00	× _____	= _____
What Happens When You Praise the Lord			
(3 tapes by Pauline Harthern)	$15.00	× _____	= _____
How to Develop Your Own Ministry			
(3 tapes by Roy Harthern)	$15.00	× _____	= _____
Church Growth			
(4 tapes by Roy Harthern)	$20.00	× _____	= _____
Church Growth through Fellowship Groups			
(4 tapes by Roy Harthern)	$20.00	× _____	= _____
How to Deal with Rejection			
(4 tapes by Roy Harthern)	$20.00	× _____	= _____
Deliverance			
(4 tapes by Pauline Harthern)	$20.00	× _____	= _____
Successful Living, Series #1			
(6 tapes by Roy Harthern)	$25.00	× _____	= _____
Successful Living, Series #2			
(6 tapes by Roy Harthern)	$25.00	× _____	= _____

gift to the ministry _____

I want to be a monthly supporter in the amount of _____

TOTAL DONATION _____

Make checks payable to Roy Harthern Ministries. (All donations are tax deductible. All material is sent postage paid.)

Your Name_____

Street _____

City _____

State_____ Zip_____

Send check and this coupon (or copy) to:
Roy Harthern Ministries
P.O. Box 3786
Longwood, FL 32779-2006